WAITING ON THE OUTSIDE

MY SON'S JOURNEY TO FEDERAL INCARCERATION AND A WHITE SUPREMACIST PRISON GANG

SHARRON GRODZINSKY

—៕—

This entire story is true. The names of people and the names of some of the places have been changed to protect the privacy of the people involved.

—៕—

ISBN: 1511682140

ISBN 13: 9781511682145

To the unknown and often misunderstood families and loved ones of inmates all over the world: may you find solace in knowing you are not alone. I hope and pray your loved ones will see the light and find their way through the darkness, pain, and suffering they have lived in and shared with you all their lives.

TABLE OF CONTENTS

1 Prison · 1

2 Early Years · 7

3 Teenage Crisis · 14

4 Family Disintegration · 17

5 Juvenile Hall · 20

6 Camp and Psychiatric Hospital · 24

7 Skinhead Years · 27

8 Survival · 32

9 First Girlfriend · 35

10 Longest Day · 40

11 The Wedding · 45

12 Illness · 49

13 Arrest and Court · 54

14 High Desert State Prison · 57

15 The Visiting Room · 61

16 Medical Care in Prison · 66

17 Aryan Warrior Prison Gang · 71

18 The Same Problems · 76

19 Coming Home · 82

20 FBI Arrest and Incarceration · 86

21 RICO Trial · 92

22 RICO Case Documents · 100

23 FCI Tucson, Arizona and FCI Edgefield, South Carolina · · · · · · 104

24 Legacy of Abandonment · 109

25 USP Beaumont · 112

26 Letter from the Past· 118

27 Visiting USP Beaumont · 121

28 Time Marches On · 126

29 Nature Versus Nurture · 129

30 Recidivism and Release · 134

    Epilogue · 141

    Acknowledgments · 145

    Support Systems · 147

Where did I go wrong?
I never meant for it to be this way
Years pass by, it's been so long
Since I have seen the light of day

I sit alone in this cell and wish I had not strayed
I miss my family—I miss my life, it's not the same
I miss the trees, the grass...if only I had obeyed
Now my life is this lonely cell, and they don't even know my name

Where did I go wrong?
I never meant for it to be this way
Years pass by, it's been so long
That I might never see the light of day

They call me by my number
They search me, and it's all the same
They wake me from my slumber
But they don't even know my name

Tell my mother I miss her
Tell my wife I wish I could kiss her
Tell my child I love him
Tell someone...they don't even know my name

CHAPTER 1

PRISON

I turned off the highway to a wide, gray landscape. Gray buildings, gray grounds, and gray fences. I had seen prisons in films before, but real life was different. It took my breath away. It filled my mouth with bile and blurred my vision with stinging tears.

As I approached the prison, the sense of dread became oppressive. I felt unimportant and insignificant, even frightened. Small drops of perspiration formed on my forehead and soaked the back of my blouse, and even though the air conditioner was on, I was drenched in sweat within minutes. The finality of it left me struggling for air. How had it come to this? What had gone wrong? How could my child, my son, whom I had cherished so dearly, have ended up here?

I could not make any excuses for him. Michael had been an intelligent, funny, handsome child who had benefited from all the advantages of a middle-class family. He had been taught the difference between right and wrong from childhood and had been given examples to follow. Now he was a twenty-seven-year-old man incarcerated in this place of concrete, fences, and bars, and there didn't seem to be any reason for this to have happened. I had been over this ground before, countless times before. The *why*, the *what if*, the *what could I have done differently* all came crashing down the day I first sat outside the High Desert State Prison in Indian Springs, Nevada.

I stopped the car on the roadside to look at what would be my son's home for the next few years, and my tears began to flow. Not your usual tears, but the kind that shake your soul and choke your breath. Tears that sting your cheeks, roll down your face, and land in your lap soundlessly. Tears that are uncontrolled, that come from somewhere you never want to know about. The kind that tell of all the sorrow and pain you feel for a child who has taken the wrong path time after time.

It had taken me forty-five minutes to get to the prison, which was off the main highway headed from Las Vegas to Beatty and northern Nevada. A bleak, washed-out desert was the only scenery along the way. Even the mountains in the distance appeared commonplace and one-dimensional. The only car on the road was mine, which made me grateful; I had wanted to make this lonely journey by myself.

When I arrived, I was surprised at the number of vehicles in the visitors' parking area. They were as varied as the worried and brokenhearted occupants they had brought to this sad place. I parked next to an old Ford pickup with an American flag in the back window. Next to the pickup was a red '57 Chevy with dice hanging from the mirror. Someone had parked a worn-out SUV in the front of the lot. I could see a child's beloved teddy bear sitting in a car seat in the back.

Who were these people who came to this place, their hopes and dreams for their family shattered by their loved one's actions and imprisonment? They are the forgotten ones. They are the ones who wait on the outside for husbands, wives, children, sisters, and brothers, while keeping up a facade of hope and happiness. They work to keep the family intact and do everything they can to keep their children from following the very same path as their fathers or mothers. At night, they sit up worrying over the stacks of bills and wondering how they will survive.

They are the ones who have borne the burden of the heartbreak and shame. They are the mothers and fathers who wonder if they did something wrong, or if they could have done something better or differently. They are the ones who feel guilty, even when they are not. I knew the story of these people...because I was one of them.

A long sidewalk led up to the main building for visitors and administration. The living area for the inmates was in the back: two-story blocks of concrete, surrounded by two rows of high electric fence with barbed wire balanced on the top, like icing on a cake. Three gun towers with 360-degree observation glass windows overlooked the grounds. I looked up at them and imagined the guards sitting up there, trigger fingers ready, aching for some infraction to happen, for someone to break the rules. A dirt road just inside the fence circled the prison so the security truck could patrol the area. The grounds were covered with gravel and lost chances.

I opened the car door to the heat of Nevada's midsummer desert. It was a heat that stung your throat and dried tears, even before they could fall.

Memories tumbled through my mind—images recalling experiences long forgotten. A boy telling his funniest jokes, a child wearing a cap and gown at his kindergarten graduation, a handsome teenager dressing for a night out, a lonely boy in a mental hospital ward. An angry young man sitting in juvenile hall. They came without warning, one after another, a lifetime of living in a few small moments.

I entered the building through the double doors and immediately saw the guard desk and the metal detector. Photos of past wardens adorned the walls, and metal lockers lined one side of the entryway. The guards looked menacing with their protective paraphernalia, radios, Tasers, and handcuffs. With shaking hands I wrote my name, address, and whom I was visiting and then signed a declaration of consent to search my person.

I knew authorities had designed the rules to prevent visitors from bringing in drugs or weapons, but who did they think I was? A drug dealer? A murderer? I was just a mother with a child in prison. A nobody with nothing to hide. A middle-class, middle-aged woman who had spent an entire lifetime trying to make sure her child got the right opportunities to follow his dreams. Now I would spend another lifetime trying to figure out what had happened to those dreams.

The female guard's badge stated that she was a Nevada Department of Corrections employee. "Mrs. Julie Jamison, who are you visiting today?" she asked.

Ashamed, looking down at my feet, I barely whispered my son's name, as if she would pass judgment on me. I had to say his name twice before she understood.

I moved through the metal detector and then stood arms and legs spread wide, while her practiced hands searched but did not violate my person. After my pat-down, she directed me to the next door, which was six feet by three feet of solid steel and could be opened only by a guard with a key. I handed my driver's license to the next guard for an identity check, and then put my hand up into a small window so the guard could stamp it. Once it was stamped, I placed it under an ultraviolet light so he could check to make sure the mark was visible. He led me into a short passageway to the next steel door and then out to a long, open walkway leading up to the visiting room.

Prisoners walked like ghosts in the heat and grayness of the yard. Some rode on a work truck, bandannas covering their heads, sunglasses glinting in the sun. They stared at me, each with their own thoughts. My shoulders drooped. I knew my son was now one of them, and it scared me. Wiping away tears with my hands, I hung my head as I walked down the sidewalk across the yard. I felt like a prisoner, a prisoner who had committed a crime, even though I had not.

The minutes passed by slowly, as if they were hours. The heat was oppressive. I prayed I wouldn't faint. The door to the visiting room was locked, so I stood in the sun and waited, not knowing there was a buzzer. Finally a guard noticed me and let me in.

The visiting room reminded me of a school cafeteria: large, with plain plastic tables and chairs. Inmates and their families had already taken up most of the tables. Some sat with a girlfriend, some with a parent or friend, and some with their wives and children. They all acted as if this was just another ordinary day. Some of them even looked happy. I couldn't understand how they found happiness in this bleak and dismal place.

I tried not to look conspicuous, or like I didn't know what I was doing. I went up to the desk, which was perched high in the corner so the guards could observe the entire room. They asked me whom I was seeing. Again the tears began, and I could hardly get his name out of my mouth: "Michael Jamison."

They motioned me over to an empty table and I sat down to wait. The tears would not stop. I did not have any Kleenex, so I used my sleeve to wipe them away, trying to get control before Michael arrived. Minutes passed. The table was wet with missed tears. I sat with my hands folded in my lap and stared, occasionally taking fugitive glances at the door where the inmates came in. The guards ignored me and kept surveying the room.

After a few minutes, the door from the prison anteroom opened, and Michael came in smiling. How could he be smiling? I couldn't even control my emotions.

We embraced and I gave him a mother's hug, long and warm. He hugged me back in a bear grip. It felt like months since we had seen each other. He almost seemed like the child so long ago left behind. Nevertheless, I knew he was not a child anymore. It made me sad.

"Mom, why are you crying?" he asked.

"I don't know. I can't seem to stop."

He waited while I wiped the tears away.

"Hey, at least you know where I am now, and you don't have to worry every night."

"For the first time in years, really," I said, thinking of all the long days and nights I had spent waiting for a phone call to tell me he was dead. All the years I waited, worried and afraid. Now the time I had dreaded had finally come, and he was not a boy anymore, but a man in prison.

I barely recognized this man sitting in front of me as my own son. He was wearing the standard High Desert State Prison blue denim shirt and pants. Both were clean and neat, but a little large on him, even though he had a stout build. He had shaved his head clean and had a goatee, which bothered me. It looked so...old. His hands were clean and he had bitten his nails to the quick, as always. I had long felt his nail biting was a physical symptom of his nerves. He was tapping his foot, too—another sign. His gray-green eyes seemed to be cooler somehow, and it looked as though he had added prison tattoos to the colorful ones he had already had before. One said "Mama's Boy" just where you could see it above his collar. Even his fingers were tattooed with the Las Vegas telephone area code, so that everyone would know where he came from.

Prison tattoos are used not just for decoration, but to let other prisoners know who you are, where you came from, and whom you are affiliated with. Michael's muscular arms were covered with gang insignias, and as I looked at them, my heart sank. I recognized that they included signs for the Aryan Warriors, a prison gang originating in the Nevada state prisons as an offshoot of the Aryan Brotherhood in California. The gang was known for its violent tendencies and belief in white supremacy, and I was devastated to see he had become a member. If he were not my son, I would have been afraid of him.

How could this have happened to the little boy I had watched play soccer and ride a bike to school? Where did it all go wrong? Where did all the lost opportunities go? How had I become the mother of not only a prisoner, but also a white supremacist gang member? I looked closely at this man, my son, and wondered how life would be from now on.

CHAPTER 2

EARLY YEARS

It was cool that winter day when I first went to pick up Michael. I pulled up my collar against the wind as I approached the flat, nondescript building next to the North Las Vegas Kmart. But though it looked so forgettable, it was the most important building of my life that day. It housed the Nevada Department of Health and Human Services, the Division of Child and Family Services, and my hopes and dreams for the future.

I walked in through the double doors and found the room where I was supposed to meet the caseworker. It was an incredibly ordinary setting. The walls were painted beige, the ceiling pale white, and the narrow corridor a dirty ivory. The caseworker greeted me with a limp handshake and a small, shy smile. He was exactly how I had envisioned a government worker should look. He was small and thin, and wore wire-rimmed glasses, plain Dockers, and a button-down shirt. I admired his dedication, but he was not outgoing or personable. He just attended to business. He sat down and pushed the paperwork toward me for the final signature.

Then another social worker brought Michael in, and the experience suddenly became extraordinary. The room brightened, and I could see he was a beautiful child. He was "baby" chubby with big hazel eyes and a generous chin. His little hands were waving in the air as if to say, "Here I am!" Only six weeks old, he was healthy and perfect in every way, and I could not have been more ecstatic. The adoption process had been held up for some additional paperwork, and the wait had seemed like months when it was only weeks.

After I finished signing the few papers and without much other fan-fare, I took him home in a beat-up old green Volkswagen bug. My husband was traveling with his band, so he was not there for that first day, but I didn't care. I had our son, and nothing else mattered.

Michael was a happy child. We loved him as our own. Old photographs show a little boy with his arms around his dog, or sitting up on his father's shoulders, or at the zoo, or in the snow, hardly able to stand up. Because his father was in a band, we traveled all over the United States and Canada and spent many hours in the back of nightclubs, listening to band rehearsals, and days on the road, traveling to the next gig. It was a magical time in the music world. Elton John was just coming into his prime with "Tiny Dancer." The Sammy Davis Jr. song "Mr. Bojangles" kept playing in our heads day after day. Three Dog Night had a hit with "Jeremiah was a Bullfrog." Who knew a song about a frog would be so popular? Chicago was the biggest instrumental band in records, and bands on the road and in Las Vegas were called "show bands." They wore velvet coats and colorful ruffled tuxedo shirts. The band my husband was in was one of those, and he was the lead singer. They were at the top of their game.

In between gigs, the three of us would go to see the zoos, parks, and museums in every town we visited. Everything was new to Michael, and he laughed and gestured with chubby baby fingers at every animal he saw. He loved going to the parks and playing on the jungle gyms and spinning roundabouts. The museums were not as exciting for him, but were interesting and fun for all of us as a day trip.

I spent a lot of time with Michael on a one-on-one basis, so he began talking at a young age. I often said he never stopped talking from his very first words. He was a real chatterbox. By the time he was four, he knew the words to half the current songs and could hold a conversation with any adult. Sometimes at rehearsals he would sing along with the band, and if they stopped in the middle of a song to revise the music or beat, he would just keep singing the words until they started again. They would laugh and say that Michael was the real director of the band.

Being on the road is not always the glamorous adventure many think it might be. It is long days of driving and even longer nights. It is another small hotel room and another new town, far away from your family and friends. We realized this was not the perfect way to raise a child, so when Michael was four, we decided to settle somewhere so he could go to school. That place was Las Vegas. It was also somewhere my husband thought he could find work.

We purchased a home in a tract of hundreds of homes on the very outskirts of the city. Now it is one of the oldest neighborhoods in Las Vegas, but back in the seventies it was an ordinary neighborhood, and what we thought was a great place to bring up a child. The house wasn't a mansion, but it was new—a four-bedroom house with eighteen hundred square feet of living area. I can still see its dreadful orange shag carpeting, bland off-white walls, and the brick fireplace in the living room. Michael had his own room, decorated with the usual little boy stuff—blue stars and stripes. Best of all, we had a corner lot with a big yard for Michael to play in, and after our block there was only the dry, arid desert. We thought we were the luckiest people on earth. We had the desert at our beckon and the night sky for a backdrop.

Unfortunately, our dreams and expectations would soon end. My husband spent the next few months job hunting, but was not able to find anything in the music business, and he was not qualified to do anything else. He did not really want to do anything else, either. Finally he decided to start a new band and go out on the road again for a few months. He was hoping he could save enough money to return and make a start again in Las Vegas.

Funny, but he never really came back. Six months went by and he just called and said he wasn't coming home. I filed for divorce, and that was the end of that.

It is easy to make this sound simple now, but it was not at the time. I was a single mother with a high school education, no job, and a four-year-old child to support. It was terrifying and heartbreaking. I cried for days. I was confused and hurt. After a lot of anger and then a lot of soul searching, I pulled myself together. Michael was counting on me; I would have to do what I needed to do to take care of him.

We spent the next few years in survival mode. My mother, stepfather, and brothers came to live with us, and thank God for that; without them, I don't think I would have survived as well as I did. We did anything and everything to keep the bills paid. I drove an ice cream truck in the desert heat during the day, and we even had a newspaper route at night. We delivered the papers from an old yellow Volkswagen van. I usually drove while my stepfather threw the papers, but sometimes my mother would drive, and I would run through apartments, making deliveries. At the end of the evening my body and clothes would be covered in dirty black printer's ink. I'd have to take a shower to get it off.

I hated getting up in the middle of the night to make sure we delivered the papers on time. I hated the dirty newsprint and the smell of ink even more. But in a strange way, that job was probably the best thing that could have happened. It was the turning point that made me realize I needed an education.

With my family's help, I began working nights in a casino and going to school during the day to become a registered nurse. It wasn't easy, and there were times when I did not know how it would turn out. However, I was determined I would have the means to get my son an education and not live on the edge of poverty the rest of our lives. It did not take me long to realize that I had an advantage over the students who had recently graduated from high school: I had maturity and motivation. I didn't just want to succeed; I had to.

During this time, the relationship between Michael and his father consisted mostly of summer and Christmas visits. Phone calls were few and far between. Michael did not really act out, but then he did not speak much about his father, either. He would ask where he was occasionally, but never really asked any more than that. Underneath I'm sure he felt deserted and rejected. How was I to know his father would end up leaving? I hated that Michael might now feel rejected by his father, and I felt rejected too. It made me feel that somehow I had failed my child.

We were bound together by rejection and need. I knew my love for him would have to sustain him from that point on.

I sent Michael to a private kindergarten I felt would provide the best opportunities for him to learn. I was like a million other parents, thinking a good start would ensure a wonderful life and future. He was smart, and the teachers said he was far above his age in terms of communication and his grasp of what they were teaching. I was so proud. He wasn't very good with his art projects, but I taped them to the refrigerator anyway. I still have the photo of him in his little gray kindergarten graduation cap and gown, smiling and looking like a small version of a college graduate. Little did I know it would be the last graduation ceremony we would ever attend for him.

Mrs. Roberts, his first-grade teacher, sent a note home about a third of the way through first grade: "Michael can't keep still and won't be quiet during class time."

She asked me to come in and have a parent-teacher meeting with her. I was obstinate and upset. I did not want to go to the meeting, and my reaction was to put the blame on her. It must be her method of teaching, or perhaps she did not like him for some reason. She was an older woman, and I thought she was probably past her time for teaching young children. It never dawned on me that she had a lot of experience with children, and that she might be right. Blind love obscured my understanding of what was really going on.

The next year he moved to a different school, and his new teacher had no problems with him. Of course I felt I had been right about Michael; this teacher just reinforced my opinion. However, in third grade, the problems began again. I received reports of deficiencies in citizenship for Michael, and notes about poor behavior in class. Teachers told me he was not paying attention and was talking while the teacher was trying to teach the class. After that it progressed to fighting with other students and causing constant disruption.

At home I began to miss small things. At first I thought I had misplaced them, but it became obvious that he was stealing from me. My father had given me a topaz gem from Okinawa and it just disappeared, along with a ring my grandmother had given me. Later I found them among his things.

By the time he was in fifth grade, I was dreading every report from school. A pattern had formed. In the first few weeks of school, he would do well and I would get good reports. Then his behavior would deteriorate, and by spring I would be wondering if he would make it through to the end of the school year.

I began to worry more and more. I went to parent-teacher conferences and read books on behavior. I was determined he would have every opportunity to make something of himself. I was working as a nurse in a hospital, and chose the early shift so I could get home shortly after school ended. I vacillated between giving him a long leash and being very controlling. I bribed him, threatened him, spanked him, and rewarded him. I tried every method of behavior modification I could think of.

Michael was about twelve when I realized he was lying to me on a regular basis, and there didn't seem to be anything that changed his behavior. Each time I caught him, he would profess his sorrow and apologize repeatedly, and then days later do something else.

By this time, Michael's father had returned to Las Vegas because his new band had fallen apart and the agent had dropped them from his listings. He had become addicted to alcohol and drugs, and although he visited Michael occasionally, he was no help at all. I will never forget the day he showed up at a Little League game, drunk, shirtless, and reeking of alcohol. He looked old and beaten, even though he was not yet forty. I watched Michael as he leaned away from his father and cringed. His father must have sensed the rejection too; eventually he left.

The next morning I called his father and told him he was an embarrassment to us, and to never show up drunk again. If he did, I would call the police. Shortly after that incident, he left town permanently.

Michael never talked about his father leaving town, and when I broached the subject with him, he would respond in a noncommittal manner. I often wondered if all the things Michael did, and all the problems he later had, were just a test to see if someone really loved him no matter what. God only knows that it should have been proven to him over and over again.

CHAPTER 3

TEENAGE CRISIS

Michael had only been nine when I remarried, and those preteen and teenage years coincided with the new marriage and stepbrothers—my new husband's three sons. None of our children were happy with the new family, and they all seemed to do their best to end our marriage and to hate each other. The boys were given all the opportunities a child could want—good clothes, their own rooms, toys, dogs, skateboards, bikes, computers, and every gadget available—but somehow a sense of family never developed. I know John and I failed in that respect. I have never been sure exactly how or why, but we did. Maybe we never had a chance to get it right from the beginning.

Michael was not happy about the marriage or much of anything else. He appeared to be jealous and acted out by interrupting, talking loudly, and acting inappropriately. As he grew older, he began stealing alcohol and drinking when no one was around. He would replace the missing alcohol with water so he wasn't found out, but we noticed what he was doing when he watered it down too much. He also stole money and jewelry from us and from neighbors. When caught, he would profess his regret and promise to never do it again. John and I both wanted to believe him, but our trust was being eroded.

Michael fought with my husband about almost everything John tried to tell him to do. It was excruciating for me to see the people I loved the most constantly arguing and fighting. I felt torn between the two and knew both of them were suffering. His stepbrothers barely tolerated him, although the youngest and the middle one tried to relate. They had their own problems, but none of them compared to Michael's. Even when I tried to bring them all together, it would end up in chaos, with arguing, shoving, and punching. It was a constant battle to keep the boys from killing each other.

I tried hard to do everything I thought was right. I would make Michael clean his room, put him on restriction, and deny him privileges, all of which rolled off his back. By eighth grade, his performance in school had deteriorated so much that he was getting in trouble on a weekly basis. I sent him for private tutoring, which brought his reading up to a tenth-grade level, but it didn't affect his behavior. The teachers and the counselors I spoke with told me he was the most difficult child the school had ever dealt with.

Finally the school district placed him in a special school for kids who were considered high-risk troublemakers. Even there, he did not seem to make any progress. Anger was a daily experience for him; it covered him like a heavy cloak, and his only outlet seemed to be getting into more trouble or using mind-altering drugs to obliterate his feelings. Alcohol and drugs became his friends.

One evening, when Michael was only about fifteen, I got a call from the police department. They told me someone had shot my son, and I needed to get to the hospital right away. That's all they would tell me. Who would shoot him, and why? It had to be some terrible mistake. I jumped in the car and drove to the county hospital, praying that he was not already dead. My heart was thumping in my chest. My head was swimming with worry. Was he okay? Was he alive? Would he die? I was afraid to speed, yet afraid not to. My car seemed to go on its own; I was only holding on to the steering wheel for strength.

When I arrived, the nurse directed me to one of the cubicles. I found Michael lying on a stretcher, head bandaged and skin pale. My heart slowed down. I took several long breaths and asked, "Michael, are you all right? What happened?"

"Some piece of shit shot me for no reason."

"Why would someone shoot you for no reason?" I said, wanting an answer I could understand instead of this flippant reply.

"It was just a bunch of guys fooling around, and I probably mouthed off and shoved one of the guys," Michael said. He had been at the Dunkin' Donuts store across from the Red Rock movie theater where he had spent the evening. Somehow he had gotten in an argument with a local gang member, and the guy had shot him. "He had his hands in his pockets, so when it looked like he was going to draw his gun, I ran. He shot me as I was running. It's a good thing he was a lousy shot, because it just grazed my head. Really, I didn't even know I was shot until the blood started running down the side of my face. Then my friend went into the donut shop and called 911. I'm really okay."

In the end, all he had was a small scar on the top of his head. He was lucky that time, but the whole experience shook me to my soul. I did not know what to do for him, with him, or about him. I was at a loss.

I called his father to let him know what had happened. Michael still had contact with him occasionally, but visits were becoming fewer and farther in between. The last visit had ended with Michael threatening his father and grandparents and screaming obscenities at them. His grandparents lived in a small town, attended their church faithfully, and had never been exposed to anyone like Michael. They probably had no idea what to think or do. They sent him back to me to handle, and he did not have a meaningful visit with them after that. Still, I guess I hoped that after the accident his father might at least find a way to spend time with Michael and talk to him about his behavior. But he did not. All he said was that Michael was out of control. Out of control? Yes, I guess he was. I could not understand how his father could desert him even if he was a problem. Since when do you ignore the fact that you have a child? What gives you the right to just sever ties and forget your obligations?

CHAPTER 4

FAMILY DISINTEGRATION

One evening a few weeks later, we were all in the kitchen and I was making dinner. Michael was slouching against the wall, his baseball cap pulled low on his face. He and John were arguing about the hours he was keeping and his problems at school. The air was tense; Michael constantly took his anger out on my husband by making derogatory remarks, and it was wearing on all of our nerves, particularly John's. He tried to be patient, but Michael's actions kept him on edge. To make matters worse, John had had a bad day at work and was tired.

I wasn't paying too much attention to what was going on, but I knew John was yelling at Michael and trying to get his attention.

Suddenly Michael leaned over the counter, grabbed one of the kitchen knives, and started making threatening stabs in the air toward my husband. He screamed, "You aren't my father and you can't tell me what to do. You don't know crap about me anyway."

By now, Michael was sixteen and a big kid, almost five foot nine and 150 pounds, so it was frightening to see him waving the knife around. I didn't know what might happen. The other boys were sitting at the kitchen table, shrinking in their chairs. The air reeked of fear.

My husband yelled back, "Who do you think is paying the bills around here and putting food in your mouth, you little shit?"

Michael edged nearer to him, knife pointed toward his chest. "I don't give a fuck who is, and I don't need you or your money anyway. You are just a stupid Jew and I hate you."

At that, my husband grabbed his arm, pushed his knee against Michael's body, and pinned him on the floor. I stepped over to them, wrenched the knife out of his hand and called the police. Michael was so out of control that we did not have any choice. We were afraid he would hurt himself or someone else. We didn't even know if he might be suicidal at this point.

By the time the police came the fight was over, and Michael was sitting at the kitchen table, looking sullen and angry. His head hung low and he had closed his eyes. I sensed he felt I had taken my husband's side and had turned against him. He was right; I had taken my husband's side, because my son was wrong.

He did not have any concept of how hurtful his words and actions had been, or what he was doing to our family. It was a vicious circle, one without an ending that could be good. The more Michael felt left out and jealous of the relationship my husband had with his boys, the angrier and more hateful he became. None of it was true, but in his mind it was. The more Michael called my husband names and acted out, the less John was willing to deal with him. I found myself caught in the middle without a way to resolve any of it. The drama made all of our lives miserable.

In the end, instead of taking him to juvenile hall that night, the police left with the understanding that we would find Michael somewhere to go to cool off for a few days. It could be a center for substance and drug abuse or somewhere else safe. My mother thought she could help, and offered for him to stay with her for a while.

They had always had such a good relationship that we all thought it might be a viable temporary solution. They had spent a lot of time together when he was a child. She had watched him at night while I worked, and had always gone to his ball games and practices. She genuinely loved him, and he knew it and respected her. Maybe, we thought, he would behave with her.

Even Michael thought it was a good idea, or perhaps he just wanted to get the hell out of the house. It was hard to tell, but all of us, including Michael, knew we had come to the end of our rope.

CHAPTER 5

JUVENILE HALL

It wasn't long, maybe a few weeks of good behavior by Michael, before tension began to permeate my mother's house too. Michael started to run with his friends again and not show up for school, and in spite of his grandmother's efforts and ours, he began to sneak out at night. I was angry that he was causing problems for my mother. One night, several weeks after the problems began again, he started arguing with her over something he had stolen from her. She called me to come over. I felt cheated that he had abused his relationship with her. How could he? I knew she was devastated too; not only did he hurt her, but she felt like she had failed me.

When I arrived, I was so angry I was trembling. She had done everything she could to try to make a connection with him, but he had continued to do what he wanted. He had abused his relationship with someone dear to him. I drove him to juvenile hall myself, right then and there.

On the way to juvenile hall, he was quiet and sullen. I was livid. "What were you thinking? What is going on in your stubborn, stupid head?"

"I don't know, Mom. I just don't have any control, and I always think things will turn out all right. I didn't mean to hurt Grandma. I love her. I just needed money to eat."

"You needed money to eat? She feeds you three times a day, every day. That is the sorriest, lamest excuse I have ever heard out of you. We will sort this out when they let you go home."

"Please, Mom, don't take me to juvenile hall."

"There is no way in hell we aren't going to juvenile hall tonight. You have made your bed, and now you are going to have to live with the consequences."

We were silent the rest of the drive. Michael sat slumped in the seat, staring ahead into the dark. I was harboring my own dark thoughts about having sent him to live with my mother, and was feeling guilty. I was also angry with Michael for disappointing both my mother and me. It was probably the biggest disappointment out of everything we had been through so far.

I hoped that a few days in juvenile hall might scare him enough for him to change his ways. It seemed like a good idea at the time. I thought that it was our only choice, because he was so out of control; maybe it was what he needed to get him through this stage and into becoming more responsible. We got out of the car, with him trailing behind me.

On entry, a corrections officer takes the juvenile's statement. Then, after emptying the juvenile's pockets, the officer places them in a single cell with a single bunk bed. The wall of the cell facing the central officer's desk is made of glass, so they can keep watch on the young inmates. They followed this procedure as they admitted Michael to the facility.

After finishing the paperwork for Michael, I looked at him in the holding area. He was lying on the bed, his muscles tense, his head turned away from the window so I could not see his face, only his body. I knew he was lying that way on purpose. As I watched, his shoulders shook and his body heaved; he was crying. In my mind I was sure I was doing the right thing, but my heart was breaking. I kept thinking I had just made the biggest mistake of my life.

They kept him for nine days, and when he came out he promised to make a new life. We actually thought he was telling the truth, and that the stay in juvenile hall had taught him a lesson. I was optimistic that this had been a life-changing event. That he had seen what it was like to be locked up. I thought he would have been scared enough to realize it was the kind of place he did not want to go back to.

It taught him a lesson all right. After his initial surveillance for suicidal issues, he was placed in the general population, where he made friends and learned how to sniff glue and take methamphetamine. The Clark County Juvenile Detention Center was understaffed and overloaded with problem kids. During the day, the juveniles were in a recreation room together or outside in the exercise area. It was impossible for the staff to watch all of the juveniles at the same time, leaving the kids the opportunity to interact with each other and pass information and whatever else they could pass.

There was no real way Michael could have gotten any help in there. Although I had thought I was doing the right thing, my gut feeling had been right. Juvenile hall was just another step toward a life of sorrow.

The court arranged for Michael, my husband, and me to go to therapy when he returned to live with us. Even John agreed to participate in the counseling sessions. Considering their relationship up to that point, this was a significant step in the right direction. It seemed for a while that things might get better. Michael stayed home at night, was respectful, and helped around the house. He even interacted appropriately with his stepbrothers and my husband. We were optimistic, but he soon began doing drugs and staying out again.

Not long afterward, Michael was hospitalized in a mental health and rehabilitation facility for drug and alcohol abuse. The odd thing was that he had checked himself in.

He was out on his skateboard one evening, and he rode it to the facility and asked to be admitted. When they called us and told us what he had done, I was astounded and hopeful, because he had taken the initiative himself. I never did find out what prompted him to check himself in, but he must have been at the end of his rope to get himself admitted without provocation from the authorities or from us.

Michael spent a month at the facility, and we had weekly family meetings to work out our problems with him. The counselors provided him with lots of tools to help him cope with his ongoing anger and addiction problems. They promoted something similar to a twelve-step program tailored for teens. However, we did not feel that, even after thirty days in rehab, he had changed enough to live with us. He still seemed sullen and angry most of the time. He slouched around the house, watching TV and glaring at everyone. He continued to carry around his anger and seemed to treat it as if it was a life raft. Maybe it was.

CHAPTER 6

CAMP AND PSYCHIATRIC HOSPITAL

I was hoping to find a way keep him away from his friends and break the cycle of drug and alcohol abuse. Because Michael had always liked the outdoors, I decided on a camp in Utah for troubled teens. I thought this approach might be better than the inpatient hospital treatment we had tried and felt had not been as successful as we had hoped.

The camp was on a ranch in a small, mostly Mormon town. It took us about six hours to get there, and throughout the journey Michael sat still in his seat, barely responding to my conversation or questions. When we arrived, we both were stunned at the appearance of the camp. The buildings looked dreary and worn. It had been raining, so the yard was full of mud. We didn't see anyone around; it did not even look like there was anything going on at the camp. I was having second thoughts. What kind of a place had I brought him to? Would this end up being another mistake?

A counselor met us at the gate and listened to our story with such passion that it took just a few minutes to convince me this was still the best option for Michael. The counselor was young and soft-spoken, yet seemed very firm in his conviction that the program would help. He told us several stories of their recent successes and offered to have us meet some of the counselors and participants. Some of their former clients, he said, had even returned to be counselors.

There were segregated sleeping quarters for girls and boys, and daily counseling for drugs, anger management, and what the counselor called "inability to function in normal life." All the general meetings took place in a large central hall, and there were several buildings for sleeping and several for counseling services. One of the buildings stored camping equipment for their trips out into the woods. There were also horses they would be riding both in the camp and out to the mountains, which is where I felt Michael would derive the most help. The entire area was fenced, and in spite of the look of the place I felt, for the first time in a long time, that this place might be able to help Michael. It was the one-on-one outdoor activities that impressed me the most. I stayed until he was settled in, and then drove the long road home alone.

I thought a lot about Michael on the way home. How his life had derailed. How my life and my family's was in chaos. I wondered again if I was doing the right thing. I second-guessed everything I had ever done for him. Should I have not remarried? Should I have not sent him to my mother's house? Should I have not taken him to juvenile hall? Should we have moved from Las Vegas? And what if I had not done any of those things? Maybe it would have turned out even worse. What if he had hurt himself or others? What could I have done differently or better? Sadly, I had no answers, no matter how much I tried to make sense of the whole thing.

All his life we had made sure to let him know he was a special, wanted child and that we loved him. We had been honest with him and had told him as a child that he was adopted, but that he would never be taken back or left alone, no matter what. Were we wrong to handle it that way? Who knows? We felt that if he found out later, as he most likely would, it would be more damaging to him than if we let him know from the beginning.

Maybe the traits he had developed were a reflection of genetics. Maybe he was programmed from the start to have the personality and problems he did. It all came down to the age-old question of nature versus nurture, and in Michael's case, I could never really say. Maybe

I should have tracked his biological mother down to see what she was like as an adult. Maybe I should have tried to find his biological father. I don't know. With the strict Nevada privacy regulations in those long-gone years, there was no way to trace his parents or find out where they were, let alone contact them. All I knew was that his sixteen-year-old mother had been only a child herself. I imagined her parents had wanted her to have the opportunity to finish high school and start a new life. I imagined how scared she must have been. She had made the ultimate sacrifice and given him up so he could have an emotionally and financially stable life with parents who loved him.

The counselors at the ranch did not allow the kids contact with anyone outside the camp for the first week. After that, they could make phone calls. The camp allowed visits after thirty days, and when I arrived after the first month, Michael seemed happy and appeared to be drug-free. He talked a lot about how much he liked the counselors and how much he enjoyed the camping trips. His counselors reported that he loved the outdoor activities, was opening up in counseling, and was getting along well with the other kids. I thought that maybe this was the answer, and that with his counselors' help and encouragement he might make a turnaround.

Then during the second month, I got a telephone call from the camp, telling me they were transferring Michael to a psychiatric hospital in Salt Lake City. He had stolen their tractor and slashed the tires, resulting in about $2,000 worth of damage. They told me they had never had a kid they could not break before. They had made him dig a ditch four feet wide and four feet deep. Then they made him fill it in and dig it up again. This had lasted most of an entire day. They had counseled him and monitored him. They had taken him up into the mountains and camped with him on a one-on-one basis. Nothing seemed to faze him or make a difference. I felt like I had used up all the options available to me and had no idea what to do next. All I knew was that another effort to find a solution had failed.

CHAPTER 7

SKINHEAD YEARS

At the hospital in Salt Lake City, the physicians finally gave him a diagnosis: conduct disorder. Conduct disorder is a psychiatric term that describes a person who cannot follow the rules, and who constantly does whatever they want to do regardless of the consequences. At last I had a name for what was wrong with Michael, and it felt like I might be better equipped to address his problems. But I still did not know why he had it. And what was the cure? No one could tell me, and certainly no one seemed to know how to treat it. The physicians at the institution told me there were some therapeutic activities that might help, like family therapy or behavior modification camps, but we had already done those things in one form or another. Looking back on the hours and hours we had spent in therapy and the money we had spent, I felt frustrated and alone, without anywhere else to turn.

The doctors released him on Ritalin, a central nervous system stimulant prescribed primarily for ADHD. He only pretended to take the pills. I found them in a sock during one of my rigorous searches for drugs in his room. When I asked him about them, he said they made him too nervous, so we threw them out. I wasn't sure if it was the right medication for him anyway; the psychiatric hospital had not kept him long enough to see if it made a real difference for him, and he had not taken it since leaving. I was also worried that without professional monitoring, it might be dangerous. They had not provided us with a follow-up plan. In the long run, it was better we did not keep the medication around the house, rather than risk him hurting himself by taking it all at once.

Around this time, he stopped attending school completely. If he left for school he would not arrive, and I would not be able to find him anywhere. Even if I took him to school and watched him enter the school, he would exit by another door. He would spend his days at other kids' houses while their parents were not at home, or he would wander alone out in the desert. The school system seemed to have given up on him, because I no longer got truancy calls from them even though he was still at an age where he was required to attend.

Within weeks of his return from the psychiatric hospital, he had run away and hooked up with an offshoot bunch of skinheads. They were part of a group of young white supremacists that originated sometime in the 1960s. By the 1980s the movement had become popular with kids who had problems with family and school relationships. The group would take them in, call them family, and welcome them as if they were their brothers and sisters. I did not know it then, but it would be the beginning of his long affiliation with skinheads and white supremacists. For reasons I have never been able to fathom, he found them fascinating as a teenager. While our family was falling apart, he took them as his "family."

Eventually I learned that they survived by rolling drunks, robbing houses and stores, and raiding 7-Elevens. When they weren't stealing, they wrote anti-black and anti-Jewish propaganda and distributed hate materials. They drove around the country to participate in demonstrations, and in general wreaked havoc on others.

I was humiliated, mortified, and deeply saddened. My son had grown up with kids of all races as friends. He was a child who had been taught to judge people for themselves, not by the color of their skin. A child who had a Jewish stepfather who had done everything he could to tolerate my son's abuse. Michael called the skinheads his family and said they cared about him. I asked him what the hell he thought I had been doing all these years.

I hated what he was doing, but I was so desperate to keep track of him and make sure he was alive that I would meet him in a park on one side of town or another and give him something to eat just to make sure he was okay. He had shaved his head by now, and he wore the skinhead uniform: a white T-shirt, black jeans, red braces, and military-style Doc Martens boots. The laces in the boots were always red, signifying he was a skinhead. He even had tattoos on his arms and chest. I was shocked at how he had changed, but I knew that if I reacted too strongly, he would get satisfaction from it. I did not want that. I felt all of this was a subterfuge designed to hurt and disgrace my Jewish husband and myself.

One day during this period of stress and fear, I was sitting at home and saw a news report about an anti-Semitic skinhead march on Convention Center Drive. I knew in my heart that he would be there, so I got in my car and drove like a maniac to where the march was. I was hoping that at least I could prevent him from appearing on television with his so-called friends.

Michael was standing at the edge of the group, participating in the chants and waving his arms in unison with the others. My anger took over. I walked right up behind him, grabbed him by the back of his shirt, and whispered in his ear, "If you don't leave with me right now, I will yell for the police and let them know you are underage." He turned and looked at me with surprise that I was even there, never mind that I was collaring him. He apparently never expected me to find out what he was doing because he knew I didn't like or take an interest in the skinhead movement.

He left with me grudgingly, but it was not the police he was afraid of; he didn't want his friends finding out he was not even seventeen yet. On the way home, he jumped out of the car at a stoplight. I did not hear from him for several weeks.

The jealousy and anger he harbored continued to drive him away, both mentally and physically. He disappeared for weeks at a time and would only call asking for money, which I refused to send. Now it was apparent he was using more and more drugs, and the things he was doing to get those drugs were more desperate.

I truly felt like I had lost him, and there wasn't anything I could do about it. It was heartbreaking for me to listen to other parents raving about how well their children were doing—how they were applying for college scholarships, had played in the last football game, were headed for law school, or were getting married. I put on a plastic, smiling face, but when I found myself alone later, I would break down and cry.

I kept asking myself what had gone wrong, and if I should have done something differently. My relationship with my husband deteriorated. He began to hate Michael for everything he had done to us. We did not talk about it, and we shared a bed with an imaginary line drawn down the middle, as if there were a wall between us. We were a family divided and a family at war.

I could not function without breaking down. I wasn't able to work, and I cried at anything at all. I refused to watch the news and stayed in the bedroom for hours on end. Sometimes I hid in the closet, just because it felt safe. My hair hung in dark clumps and strands would come out when I brushed it, and my skin grew sallow. I did not want to do anything except stay home in bed and feed my depression as if it were an animal.

I could not think of anything I could do about my son, and although my husband was usually supportive of me, he wanted nothing to do with Michael. Then one day I realized I couldn't do anything myself. Michael was the only one who could change the direction he was taking.

Now my nights were spent lying awake, either sobbing or waiting in dread for the police to call and tell me he was dead or in jail.

One evening months later, the telephone did ring late at night, and it was Michael. He was crying and said he was in Phoenix and was starving. "I know what I have been doing is crazy, and I only did it to get back at you for marrying someone. I don't really belong here and I need help. Please come and get me. I haven't had anything to eat for days and days. This whole skinhead thing was a big mistake, and I want to come home."

The fact that my husband was Jewish, he said, had just given him somewhere to focus his hate. I believed his story, caved in, and sent him a bus ticket home.

Later he admitted that what really had happened was that he had fallen out with the skinheads. They had tossed him out after using him as a pawn, a strong kid who had been willing to do their bidding. Still, I couldn't let go of my own secret hopes that he had seen the light and would somehow change into the child I had envisioned for so many years.

Shortly after he came home, we had a long talk about all his problems. I asked him for the hundredth time why he continued to do these things, even though they made his life miserable.

He looked directly at me and said, with tears filling his eyes, "Mom, do you really think I want to be this way?"

I was dumbfounded. All this time, I had thought he enjoyed the drama and the conflict. Sometimes I had thought he was doing things on purpose to keep attention focused on him, and to make life miserable for my husband and me. His problems had taken up so much of my energy for so many years that I guess I had just stopped thinking about what he might be going through. The revelation that he really did not want to be like he was, and have all the problems it created, made me realize that his chances of making significant changes for himself were not good. Maybe he did want to do the right thing, but he was never able to maintain normalcy for any length of time. He would get caught up with other people and their problems, rather than taking care of his own, and those people and problems always led to drugs and illegal activities. Why he would put others before his own family became an ongoing question that was never answered. Even though I felt I understood him better, I still had no solution.

CHAPTER 8

SURVIVAL

When he was seventeen, I gave Michael a choice: finish school or get a job. The school district regulations stated that a child did not have to go to school after they reached seventeen, which was a relief, as school was no longer a legal problem I had to worry about. But he had to do something other than just stay home or wander around with friends. He said he wanted to work, but never got a job.

At my wits' end, I finally got him into the car and took him up to Idaho for a survival course. I had heard about it from friends who'd had positive results for their troubled teens. The program said they had a very high rate of success with even the most difficult kids. After all the trouble we had in Utah and his running away and joining the skinhead group, I thought he would certainly qualify as "difficult." Luckily, he liked the idea and was looking forward to it.

I dropped Michael off at the survival course weighing 150 pounds, and when I picked him up two weeks later, he weighed just 125. During the course, he wrote me letters telling me how much he had learned about himself, how this was changing his life, and how the skills he was learning would enable him to live a normal life in the community:

—⁂—

Mom, this is the hardest thing I have ever done. They make you hike all day and only give you a handful of rice and a few raisins to eat.

They expect you to trap and kill everything else. I'm even thinking about eating bugs, I am so hungry. All I dream about is a nice, big, juicy hamburger and fries. Tomorrow we are going to try to catch a snake and eat it.

After hiking all day, we have to dig out our bed, find some branches to soften it, and lie down with just the thin blanket and poncho they gave us. If it is really cold, we have to make a fire with coals, put them in our bed, cover them with dirt, and then lie down on top of the dirt. Otherwise, I think we would freeze to death. This is really going to teach me how to survive when I get home. I miss you very much and can't wait to see you.

Love, Michael

—w—

At the end of the survival course, I drove back to Idaho to pick him up. I met him in a broad, flower-filled field. It was a beautiful, clear day, the kind that you tend to remember and savor for a long time. The colors of the field were vibrant with early spring wildflowers, and the setting sun cast long shadows over the purple hills, descending behind the survival group as they came over the mountain. It seemed like the perfect end for his course, and the perfect pathway to a new beginning.

As the group of teens and counselors came closer, I did not even recognize my own son. He looked so worn, tired, thin, and dirty in his poncho and jeans. Nevertheless, he had a new strength in his face, and the way he carried himself showed a self-confidence that I hadn't seen before.

After we parents hugged our kids, the whole group formed a circle in the open field. They clasped hands and sang a song. Then each participant gave a demonstration of what they had learned. They could start a fire without matches. They could find food in the wild and cook it. They had caught snakes and mice, and had eaten them along with their meager portions of rice and raisins. They had hiked ten miles a day. They had endured extreme weather, almost freezing temperatures at night and the hot sun during the day. Filled with enthusiasm and self-confidence, they looked like they could take on the world. They were drug-free and had not smoked in two weeks. They were on their way to a new life.

Michael was starving, so on the way home we stopped at a 7-Eleven to get him some snacks. While I was paying for the snacks, he stole a pack of cigarettes. I only found out about it during therapy sessions much later down the road.

CHAPTER 9

FIRST GIRLFRIEND

When Michael turned eighteen, my brother found him a job laying block. I was grateful my brother had done this for him; my family had always been supportive of me, even though they knew Michael was difficult. I felt lucky to have their support and generosity.

And Michael appeared to be settling down and becoming responsible for himself. He had not been in trouble for some time since the survival course, and I felt comfortable with how he was acting. My fears began to subside.

Since he was working and seemed to be making an independent life for himself, I let him rent a small house we owned nearby. He seemed to be happy in his new home, and my brother said he showed up on time and worked hard all day. In fact, Michael was good at his job and was not causing any problems at work or with us. He even began a serious relationship with his first real girlfriend.

Jennifer was a bright, outspoken, attractive girl with short blond hair and a small heart tattooed on her right shoulder. She seemed mature, even though she certainly had her own family problems. She also had issues with some minor drug use; in fact, they had met in one of his drug rehab programs. I walked a fine line between hoping this was a good thing for him and being afraid that he would revert to his old habits.

Still, she was much more of an adult than Michael was, and I harbored hopes she would help keep him out of trouble. For quite a while, it did seem like things were going well. They continued to have a happy relationship. He kept his job. They came to dinners at our home together, and Jennifer fit so well with the rest of the family that she became someone we looked forward to seeing and being with. It was a relationship that brought us all together—one that we all needed so much.

One evening Michael and Jennifer came to the house for dinner and told us she was pregnant. Not that anyone was surprised; they had been careless, as many other young people had been. It was not the worst thing he'd done. I even thought it might be good for him. Maybe having his own child would give Michael that sense of family and belonging he had so desperately been seeking. He would not be the only young person who made a complete change when the right person and a family came along.

My grandson was born on Thanksgiving Day. When Jennifer started her labor, they called me to take them to the hospital. After we arrived, they took her into a room to prepare her. I waited, pacing and worrying, for nearly ten hours while Jennifer struggled with the birth. Michael alternated waiting with me and sitting with Jennifer. He was supportive of her, but like most new fathers, seemed fearful of what was to come. When the nurses finally told me they had a beautiful baby boy, I cried tears of relief. It felt like a miracle.

After Danny was born, there was a period of calm and contentment for all of us. It was especially apparent in the way Michael loved and held his son. My husband, who still disliked Michael, loved Jennifer and loved his grandson, too. There was just a glimmer of hope in my heart that we might achieve some kind of family reconciliation.

But although I thought everything was okay, it was not. Michael soon began to stray, use drugs, and hang around with the wrong type of people again. Within three months after Danny was born, those old habits began to surface. Michael started missing work, and the arguments between him and Jennifer, which they had been trying to hide, were now very apparent. I had to help with buying groceries and diapers because there was not enough money. The house was a mess, and there were always people coming in and out or camping on the floor. Some of them stayed for days, leaving Jennifer to take care of the baby and clean up after them.

Finally, when Danny was about nine months old, Jennifer took him and went to Hawaii to live. I did not blame her for leaving. She knew that the best thing for her child would be to get him away from the environment they were living in. Nevertheless, it was as if someone had taken a part of me, and there wasn't a thing I could do. There was no good solution other than the one she had chosen.

Michael professed unhappiness when Jennifer left with the baby, but he continued all his activities as if everything was okay. One day a few months after she left, I drove by the house and confronted him and his friends. They all looked disheveled and stoned, just sitting around watching music videos, smoking cigarettes, and dropping ashes all over the floor. There were about six of them in the living room, mostly young. One of them, a hulking kid about twenty-five, tried to stare me down. I was so furious I didn't even think to be scared. I looked straight at Michael. "Who the hell are these people?"

"Just friends. Don't get your panties in an uproar." He sneered at me as if I were some kind of irritating bug.

The house was filthy. Garbage overflowed the trash can and junk was piled on the porch. The vertical blinds in the kitchen were bent and broken, hanging like pieces of ragged linoleum. One of the kitchen chairs had a leg missing, and cigarette ashes covered the coffee table. Even the walls were dirty.

"Get the hell out of this house right now before I call the police. This house belongs to me. I want you all out right now."

Slowly they got up and shuffled toward the door. Most of them just left, but one or two of them challenged me with looks of contempt.

All the while Michael was saying, "You don't really have to go. She's just mad and she'll cool down."

"No, dude," said the big kid. "We're out of here."

After they left, Michael asked, "Why did you have to go and do that? We weren't doing anything."

"Weren't doing anything? Are you insane?" He and his friends had trashed the house—the house that was supposed to be for him, Jennifer, and the baby. Now that Jennifer and Danny were gone, it was a disaster. "The bathrooms are filthy. There's garbage all over, and the place hasn't been cleaned in months. Are you even working?" I demanded.

"Of course I'm working," he said, obviously trying to calm me down. "I've been at work every day this week. You can call if you want to." His eyes darted up and to the left. I knew he was lying.

Frustrated and angry, I left. I drove around the block and came back to check if anyone had been lurking in the area and had come back to the house. The blinds were closed, so I went home.

From then on, it was a downhill slide for Michael. He let a kid draw wildly extravagant graffiti on the block wall of the backyard and bedroom walls of the house. I almost cried when I saw the drawings. Michael thought they were "way cool," but I did not. I knew he had destroyed the property and ruined his chances of getting a job again. We fought about it daily, by phone or when I came over to try to reason with him. Each time I came close to throwing him out, he would back off or do something to make me hold off again. One time he said he had a good job and had started working. That turned out to be a lie, or else he never showed up for the job. Another time he cleaned up part of the house and yard and promised to finish the rest. He did not, of course.

By now I realized that his childhood diagnosis of conduct disorder had been correct. It was evident from his resistance to all authority figures, his failure to realize some of the things he did were wrong, his lack of remorse, his lack of respect for others and their feelings and needs, and his continued manipulation of those around him to get what he wanted.

I knew I had been manipulated repeatedly, but my desire to help when he asked with sincerity always afforded him an edge that would get me to go along with his program. In our therapy together, I had learned to maintain a purposeful direction of holding my ground, and to correct his rude comments and demands. But I had not learned to resist completely. I was weak from my desire to have a child who loved others and could get along in life, one I could be proud of. His failures were mine. Throughout the years, we had performed a dance that never changed in essence; just in the way the steps were performed. Both of us contributed to the dance and the music.

CHAPTER 10

LONGEST DAY

Later that summer, I handed down an ultimatum: clean up or get out. When he did not do either, I phoned to tell him I was coming over. "I'll be there in ten minutes, so get your stuff together. I'm calling the police to have you and whoever else is there put out."

He was around twenty years old now, had quit working again, and was stealing to feed himself, snatching food from grocery stores and wherever else he could manage. On the occasions when I would come by, there always seemed to be some shiftless person hanging around the house. The house was always trashed and dirty, clothes strung all over the place. Unpaid bills stacked up until the utility companies cut off the power, then the water. I was tired of the whole thing and just wanted him out of there. The frustration had worn me down to a point where I really did not care about him, the house, or where he would go. He could live on the street for all I cared.

When I drove up, the blinds were drawn and the house looked desolate. He was sitting alone in the darkened living room. I charged into the house as angry as I had ever been, screaming, "Get out right now, or I'm calling the police." He just sat there quietly, letting me rant.

Then I saw the gun in his hand.

After a period of silence, where neither of us could speak, he said, "Mom...I can't take it anymore. I'm hooked on meth. My friends are scum. I'm just some douchebag who doesn't even have enough money to buy a loaf of bread. Life sucks."

It's hard to convey the feeling of seeing your child with a gun. The moment stretched out, an infinitude of pure terror and distress. My body trembled. My hands shook like a bird in flight. My face had gone numb except for my eyes, which felt like they were twitching out of their sockets. Waves of doubt and confusion swept over me. "Give me the gun," I heard myself say.

He raised it. "No, Mom. Life just isn't worth living anymore." And then he put the gun in his mouth. Put the gun in his mouth, just like in the movies, only it was real this time. It was real, and he was really holding a gun. My child. Even in my worst fears, in all the times I had lain awake worried, I had never envisioned something so awful. What mother could?

I stood very still and then, with every bit of determination I could summon, I spoke. "I love you very much, Michael, and I hope you won't choose to do this." I paused, weighing my final words. "But whatever you choose, I won't stand here to watch it."

I turned my back on him and walked out the door. I turned my back on him and left. To this day, I will never know where the strength to walk away came from, but I know that by doing this, I saved my son's life. By not buying into his morbid scene, I saved his life that day—and maybe my own, too.

My body was still shaking when I got into the car. The heat inside was intolerable, furnace-like, but I still felt cold. I turned the ignition key, swung the car around, and kept my eyes on the road, struggling to not look at the house, trying not to listen for the sound of a gunshot. I drove away not knowing if my son was dead or alive.

When I got home, I went right to the kitchen and sat by the phone. I was far too numb to think. I just sat there staring at nothing, waiting.

Two hours passed, and no one called. I began to come back to reality. I knew I had to call the house and see if he answered; if he didn't, I would ask the police to go over and check on him. I could not go back there myself, not after what had happened.

I stared at the phone. It felt like an object from another planet, another dimension—as though I'd never seen or used anything like it before. Ironic, I thought, considering how important it was to me on that particular morning. It was an instrument of destruction or of relief. I dialed the number with care, one digit at a time, doing my best not to think or cry.

He answered after five agonizing rings.

"Hi Mom. I guess I made it through that one..." He trailed off. "But I really need help, Mom. Can you come over?"

I told him I would be over right away. "But if you want my help," I said firmly, "you'll have to give me the gun."

"Okay," he agreed. "You win this one."

When I arrived, he handed the gun over to me. I locked it in the trunk of my car until I could figure out what to do with it. Eventually I had it destroyed so it would not be available for someone else to get into trouble with.

We both knew Michael could no longer stay in the house. Part of his problem was the friends he had made during the past few years; everyone knew where he lived, and they came and went, even if he wasn't there. They would just break into the house through the patio door if he was not home.

What he needed was rehab, but we had already exhausted all the available mental health options. Insurance companies apparently do not think people with substance abuse problems need more than a few thousand dollars' worth of treatment. The best idea we could come up with was for him to go to Laughlin, Nevada. There was a lot of new construction going on, and hopefully plenty of jobs to choose from. The work would take him away from his circle of friends and the downward spiral of his habits. He promised me he would attend Alcoholics Anonymous (AA) and Narcotics Anonymous (NA) there, too. It was a place where he might resume at least some semblance of a normal life.

We drove to Laughlin just like two people on an everyday outing. Any casual observer might have thought we were going on a picnic. Michael acted, for once, like a normal human being. No verbal abuse, no obscenities, no accusations or threats. It felt like a miracle.

"You know, Mom, if this works out like I hope—if I get a good job—maybe I could send some money to Jennifer, and maybe she will let me see Danny."

I sighed. "Well," I said, "they are in Hawaii, which is a long ways off, but if you made enough money, I suppose you could send them a ticket back here. Anyway," I added, trying to keep his expectations in line with the situation, "before you start thinking about that, you have to get yourself straight and get yourself clean. You can't accomplish anything if you aren't right with yourself."

Each time I called to see how he was doing, I hoped he would be working, so he might be able to get Jennifer and the baby to come back. But a few weeks later, I got a call.

"Hi Michael." It was the fourth time I had spoken to him since he'd moved to Laughlin. "How is it going?" I asked with a sigh.

"It's okay, Mom, but there doesn't seem to be any work for me. I go to the job sites, but they want someone who carries a union card." His voice crackled with frustration.

I had heard this before, of course, and already could see where it was going. He would not find any work and would have to come back to the same environment that prompted his flight to Laughlin.

He arranged to return and stay with a friend he had worked with in the past. I was nervous about this because I didn't know the person, but I hoped that at least being alone down in Laughlin had given him the time to think about how he'd been living, how many people he had hurt. Perhaps he also might have realized how the very friends he was so determined to help had dragged him down and been a part of all his problems.

I knew his chances on his own were slim, and although he talked about wanting to change, he would have to show a real commitment.

Michael might not ever live a completely normal life. He had lived on the dark side too long. But could he at least be a person who did the right thing? I hoped with all my heart that he could.

There wasn't anything I could do but hope.

CHAPTER 11

THE WEDDING

In his early twenties, Michael surprised us all and entered into another phase of seeming normalcy. I was cautiously happy. He had a job laying block again and seemed to be living a decent life. He was going to AA meetings, speaking to young people about drugs and alcohol, and staying sober. He was making enough money to support himself, and had even gotten a raise at work. Then another girl appeared in his life. She was tall and thin, with an innocent look about her. This girl was the one he would marry.

Erica came from a background of problems herself, although she had strong hopes for her future. She fit right into the pattern he liked: pretty, but in need of attention and love. Someone he could manipulate easily. Jennifer had learned to defend herself, but Erica was not able to resist. She fell for the attention he showered on her, his humor, his bragging, and his exaggerations of things he had done, or would do for her.

It wasn't long before she was pregnant, and they announced that they wanted to get married. I was surprised that they wanted to settle down, but since Michael seemed to be doing reasonably well, my husband and I agreed to support the marriage. Both of them were working and were saving their money to buy a few things for the baby. They had already bought a bassinet and car seat.

So that they would have a decent place to live, I had let them move into the now-repaired house Michael had destroyed before. We thought that if we agreed to help with the wedding, it might help them with their relationship, and they would have a lovely ceremony. I wanted them to have this chance, and my husband, in spite of his long-standing troubles with Michael, agreed we would provide for a small reception.

To say the wedding was unusual would be an understatement. It was held in our members' club, with a beautiful wedding arch, ribbon trimmings, and fresh flowers. The guests ranged from middle-aged professional friends of ours to longtime childhood friends of theirs, plus a handful of drug addicts and alcoholics. Most of them were in recovery and had met Erica and Michael at the AA recovery center. Some guests arrived in suits and cocktail clothing, and others in jeans and leather jackets with Harley Davidson logos. One guy even showed up in shorts, flip-flops, and his AA shirt. I accepted it, ignored it, and let it be Michael and Erica's day.

For some deep-seated reason, Michael had contacted his adoptive father and invited him to the wedding too. I don't know how he found him, but he did. They had not spoken in years. Maybe Michael had thought he might get the approval he had so long sought from his father, but that did not happen.

After the wedding, Michael and his father had some type of disagreement, and their conversation became tense and angry. It would turn out to be the last time they would see each other—the period at the end of a sentence. A finale to the music. An end to a relationship that had faltered for years.

Other than that, it was a great day and a wonderful party for everyone. No one could have asked for a more beautiful bride or handsome groom. Erica looked stunning in her lace-wedding gown with her blond hair piled high, and her dimples accentuated her wonderful smile. He had a block layer's muscular build, and his smile could light up a room. On the outside they were the picture of what every parent would want to see in their children. However, what you could not see was that on the inside, they had so many personal problems that the marriage was doomed from the start.

Several months after the wedding, their daughter, Sarah, was born, and things began to go downhill for them. There was constant fighting. Michael quit going to his NA and AA meetings and began to stay off work. The more he failed, the more he belittled Erica, calling her names and telling her how stupid she was. It was even worse than his relationship with Jennifer.

This time I stepped in. "Erica, you can't let him talk to you that way. You have to stand up for yourself or leave him, even if he is my own son. It just isn't right." I told her this one day in the kitchen. She had just spent an hour cleaning up a mess he had left on the stove and in the sink. "This place looks terrible, and he doesn't lift a finger to help you with the house or the baby. Why don't you just kick him out?"

Erica turned her head to the side as if she were thinking, or maybe just avoiding the truth right in front of her face. "I've tried, but he just says this is his house and if I don't like it I can leave." She put her cigarette out in an ashtray that was overflowing with butts. "Then he threatens to kick me out. I don't have anywhere to go."

"This is my house and it's in my name. If you want him out, call the police and I will help you get him out," I said. I was sick of how he treated her and all the lies he had been telling Erica and me. He did and said what he wanted in order to get what he wanted. She and the baby needed a safe place to stay. Michael wasn't working, and I was pretty sure he was doing drugs again. Once again his drug addict friends were in and out of the house, lying around all the time or trashing the place. "How can you live like this?" I asked, looking around at the piles of clothes, shoes, and toys. "This just isn't right for Sarah."

Erica finally kicked him out, after calling the police several times and then making up with him before the police arrived. Michael went off to stay with his so-called friends, who were as much trouble as he was. But he kept coming back to the house, and Erica just couldn't seem to keep him away. He would be full of remorse one minute and then scream awful names at her the next. The more drugs he did, the more belligerent and mean he became.

About six months after the problems began, Erica took the baby and disappeared. I did not even know where she had gone.

When he came crying to me about it, I was not sympathetic at all. "Michael, what did you expect her to do? She gave you a million chances.

All you did was argue with her. You didn't even keep a job. What did you expect?"

"Well, I thought she loved me."

"How could you think anyone could love you when you treated them the way you did? You didn't work, you treated her like she was dirt, and you didn't help with the baby. How many diapers did you change? What did you think would happen? What didn't you learn from what happened with Jennifer and Danny?"

He looked at me and said, "I love her and Sarah with all my heart. Can't you help me get them back?"

"No, Michael, I can't. That's something you will have to do yourself."

Later he found her living with a girlfriend in Fontana, California. Eventually Erica came back for a weekend and brought the baby so I could see her. I suspected he had convinced her to visit, and of course, she and Michael made up. By this time Michael had destroyed the house again, and I had told them they had to move.

They came to my office the next Monday and asked if I would give them the money to rent a truck so they could all move to Fontana. I asked them if they were out of their minds, but they said all the right things: they could get work there, they could make a new start, he would not have the temptations he had here, and things would be so much better. Eventually, because of Sarah, and like I always did when I thought they really meant it, I gave in and rented a truck for them to move to Fontana. At least now I could clean the house and sell it.

In a way, their move to California was a blessing for me. I was no longer in the middle of their arguments and problems, and I was not around the corner for them to turn to with requests for help and money. I hoped that being on his own with Erica and Sarah would help him learn to settle down and take care of his responsibilities. Maybe, away from all his drug addict friends, he would take steps toward being a good husband and a father. I knew they might have a difficult time, but it was time for him to grow up and start taking care of his family.

CHAPTER 12

ILLNESS

With Michael, Erica, and Sarah living away, I was able to focus on other things in my life. I could visit my father, who was living in northern California, and spend time with my mother, who had unfortunately become seriously ill. My stepfather had died many years before.

My mother had always been healthy for her age, but during a visit I noticed something was very wrong. She had lost so much weight I could not believe it; her arms were like sticks, her face pale and drawn, and her clothes hung on her. After many doctor's visits and tests, we found out that she had an unusual pulmonary disease called *Mycobacterium avium* complex (MAC) infection. It is very similar to tuberculosis, but it is not transmissible through the air; you cannot contract it just by being in the same room.

Because it was so hard to treat, the doctors sent her to the National Jewish Center for Immunology and Respiratory Medicine in Denver for six long weeks, and I went with her for her treatment. When she came home, she was on intravenous antibiotics for six months. Eventually she got better, only to be subsequently diagnosed with cancer of the liver.

As time passed, she became so frail that she was confined to the house. We had home health care during the day, and my two brothers and I were there every evening. Oddly enough, my father also came down to visit with her, and they spent time reliving old memories, both good and bad. It was a time of forgiveness for both of them.

During all this my husband, who had been so supportive of me for the past fourteen years despite all the grief we had endured with Michael, gave up on our marriage and decided to move on to other relationships. We sold our house and were divorced within six months. At least all the boys were out on their own, and not much of what happened between their father and me affected them. Unfortunately, it did affect me.

I lost weight and became so depressed that I no longer wanted to do anything that was fun or pleasant. I was able to perform my duties at work, but just barely. I felt as terrible as I had when Michael had joined the skinhead group and left home. The only thing that kept me going was caring for my mother.

Luckily I no longer was dealing with Michael and his problems too. They were still in Fontana, but I knew things were not going well. Their phone was disconnected most of the time, which was a relief to me. I could not have dealt with crisis calls from them in addition to my own problems. It was all I could do to get through each day as it was.

Toward the end of my mother's illness, Erica and Sarah came up to Las Vegas alone. She said she had left Michael for good. I just said, "Good for you. You know I will always support you." He had found a new source of drugs in Fontana, and in fact was cooking and distributing methamphetamine.

Erica looked thin and drawn. She said she was worried about Sarah. The last time they had visited, Sarah had been walking and trying to talk. I thought she might be a little behind, but she could say a few words like "Mama," "Dada," and "puppy." Now Sarah wasn't saying a word, and had daily episodes of crying, kicking and screaming. No amount of consoling or treats could get her to stop.

"When did she start this?" I asked during one of her fits.

"She's been doing it on and off for about three months now. Nothing I do seems to help, and I'm having a hard time dealing with it." Erica sat sideways in her chair, drawing in smoke from her cigarette and looking desolate.

"She isn't saying anything at all? What happened?"

"She just stopped talking about the same time she started having these fits. She also does not look you in the eye, and doesn't play with her toys anymore. It's almost as if she has left the planet, and I am extremely worried that something is wrong with her."

The journey to find out what was wrong with Sarah started with the pediatrician, who thought it might be something like autism and referred her to a neurologist. The neurologist took one look at her and referred her to a specialist in San Diego. He suspected she had Rett syndrome, a genetic disorder that affects only girls.

On the day of the visit to the specialist, I drove to Fontana to pick them up and found out that Michael was going too. I wasn't sure how he had found out about Sarah's illness or whether he and Erica were back together, and I didn't care. I told him, "You can go, but I don't want any trouble, and I don't want to hear a word out of either of you. Is that clear? Today is about Sarah only." The last thing we all needed was a fight between them. Sarah's health was what was important.

The specialist ordered blood work but verbally confirmed the diagnosis of Rett syndrome, a genetic neurodevelopmental disease. According to the National Institute of Neurological Disorders and Stroke[1], a particular protein called MeCP2 is transmitted to the brain at certain times during the growth process, but needs monitoring and moderation. With these special girls, the body does not moderate MeCP2, resulting in damage to the brain. The damage leaves them with severely decreased mental capabilities. In many cases, they lose their ability to speak and may have autistic-like behavior. Most of the girls also have severe physical disabilities which develop as they age, such as poor motor functions, scoliosis, decreased ability to walk, difficulty with maintaining weight, and one of the hallmark symptoms of Rett syndrome: a constant wringing of the hands. Sarah had all the classic symptoms.

After that there were more tests and trips to the doctor for Sarah, including the insertion of a permanent gastric feeding tube. Her tantrums, probably caused by pain, stopped for the most part and she became a

---

1   National Institute of Neurological Disorders and Stroke, *Rett Syndrome Fact Sheet* (Bethesda, MD: Author, 2009), http://www.ninds.nih.gov/disorders/rett/detail_rett. htm.

happy child. She was at least able to maintain her ability to walk and hand-feed herself. However, it was still a lifelong commitment, placed squarely on the shoulders of Erica.

It is hard to even imagine the strength it takes to care for a child with such severe disabilities. Most people do not know how challenging it can be, how it saps the life from you and tires you out both mentally and physically.

There are rewards in the love you get from your child, and when small advances are made, but the everyday challenges can take you down a path of despair. In addition, you know that the diagnosis includes the fact that she will never get any better. She will never go to a prom, read a book, ski, get a job, or be able to live alone. There will be more and more medical problems to deal with, along with the continuing frustration of dealing with government entities.

Without help from Michael, Erica had to go it alone. Of course the State of California and other social agencies were there to help, but where are they at two in the morning when your child is throwing up? Where are they when you are out of diapers? Where are they when the feeding tube is clogged, the medications aren't effective, or your child is coughing through the night and might have pneumonia? They are daytime agencies. You need help from someone who is right there beside you, giving you both moral and physical support. Michael, like his own father, was never there.

I had hoped Sarah's diagnosis would have been a life-changing experience for him. However, he was not able to make the leap from self-centeredness to taking responsibility for his children. He was so addicted to methamphetamine now that it was the most important thing in his life. Not only was he manufacturing it, but he was also selling it in order to maintain his habit, which was costing a couple hundred dollars a day on the street.

The police in Fontana finally caught up with him and his drug dealing. Instead of giving him jail time, the judge sentenced him to three months in a rehabilitation center in California. The jails were already crowded, so they were reducing sentences for first-time drug offenders. I wished they had kept him longer, so he could have broken his habits and learned some skills to deal with his addictions.

When he finally got out of rehab, he came home and said, "Mom, I swear to you...I am going to make a new start. I have a job back at my old place, and they will let me use the work truck. All I need is somewhere to stay."

It was the same old routine. I paid for a place for him to stay for a month. By the end of the month, he was missing work and drinking or doing drugs, or both. He became belligerent and angry when I refused to continue the rent or give him any money.

I did not see him again until my mother died several months later. At least he came to the service. It was a small, but unforgettably heart-felt outdoor memorial ceremony, with a beautiful arrangement of roses and music from an acoustic guitar to accompany her on her journey to heaven. I knew she was going to heaven if anyone was.

Michael wore a dark suit and sat through the service with his head bent down in his hands, elbows on his knees. She had been a staying factor in his life and had always tried to support him. She was the one who would tell him he could succeed no matter what. She even gave him lessons in oil painting and bought him a canvas to work with. She had let him use her car and stay with her, and she had always cooked his favorite meals. I remembered the time she sewed a leather vest for him, not knowing it was part of his skinhead uniform, but she did it for him so he would feel good about himself. He was twenty-five years old now but cried like a baby at her service, his body shaking while he sobbed, and he stayed long after we all had gone.

CHAPTER 13

ARREST AND COURT

During the next couple of years, I saw Michael occasionally, but did not provide any help for him. He had a string of odd jobs, most having to do with the seamier side of Las Vegas, and there were several stripper girlfriends. On one visit, he and his girlfriend of the moment stole my credit cards and charged a thousand dollars' worth of stuff. I never let him in my house again without out watching him every second. If he came over, I would keep anything of value locked in my bedroom. My trust was completely gone.

Meanwhile, Erica and Sarah were still in California, and I heard from them occasionally. Jennifer had finally brought Danny back to the mainland, and they were now living in a small town in Texas near her mother. Jennifer had found a great job, so I felt comfortable with what was happening with all of them.

I wasn't sure where Michael was living and only saw him infrequently. Then one day I got a call from him about four in the afternoon. I remember it because I was washing clothes and listening to the early news. He said he had spent the last week in a seedy motel on Boulder Highway, trying to come down from a three-day high. He was begging for food. I took him three cheeseburgers and a giant Coke. When I arrived, he was huddled up in blankets. He was dirty and thin as a rail, and the girl with him did not look much better. She was skeletal thin with dirty-blond hair hanging over her eyes. She had on black punk-rock clothing and wore black net stockings. Black mascara trailed down her face; she must have been crying. The shades were drawn. The TV was on some music video station playing heavy metal rock music, and there were clothes and trash strewn around. Even if there was a maid, she had not been in the room in days. I knew he was in serious trouble, but there wasn't anything I could do to help him. Any change he made had to come from him. I had known this for a long, long time, so I left.

At two in the morning a few weeks later, I got the next call from Michael. He was in the Clark County Detention Center. He had been booked on forgery, cashing forged checks, and possession and sale of methamphetamine. He called ten times that day, asking me to get him out. I refused and eventually blocked his calls. I just could not take any more of his crying and begging, and the only way to stop it was to block his calls.

The court gave him three years' probation. I could not believe it. After court I told him he had better thank his lucky stars and consider this a gift, but I didn't really think he realized how lucky he was or appreciated the fact that he had gotten a break. That is what drugs do; they change your perceptions. I left him at the courthouse with his latest girl-friend, who was also hooked on meth. She was someone who had been in and out of his life since grade school. I felt sorry for her and knew she was on a downhill slide, too. I wondered how her parents were coping, or if they had given up on her.

Less than a month later, he was back in jail for forging another check and trying to cash it at a casino. When I went to see him at the Henderson Detention Center, he looked dejected and sorry for himself. His face was drawn, and the blue detention center jumpsuit hung on his frame. He said he was sick from coming off drugs.

"Could you have been more stupid?" I asked.

"I guess not."

"You certainly didn't learn anything from the last time. I hope they send you right to prison and don't let you out this time," I said, talking into the phone connecting us through the glass partition. I sat on a plastic chair in an individual alcove, which provided a little privacy for the phone visit.

"I've got the shakes, Mom."

"Too bad. Why don't you tell them you need some medication?"

"They don't much want anything to do with guys like me."

"Then you'll just have to suffer, won't you?" I said as I thought, It serves you right, after all the misery you have caused everyone else for years. I could tell by looking at him that he was not in serious medical trouble. He would survive. Besides, the detention center had plenty of experience dealing with drug-related medical problems.

Two months later, I arrived at the courthouse for his day in the Clark County Court. After passing through the metal detectors, I went up to the second-floor courtrooms and found his case in Courtroom Six. I had heard that the judge for this session did an expert job of dealing with an enormous number of cases in a fair and efficient manner. The courtroom was packed with prisoners in their blue jumpsuits, their feet shackled together and hands chained to their waists. They filled every row in the area set aside for defendants. It was like a zoo in there that day. The judge was severely overloaded, and a great deal of the prisoners did not speak English, so they needed interpreters. It seemed like forever before the judge got to Michael's case.

When she did get to him, she asked him to say in his own words what he had done.

"I cashed a check, Your Honor."

"That doesn't constitute an offense in this state, as far as I can remember," she said. "What else did you do?"

"I guess the check wasn't mine, and I guess I signed someone else's name."

It was the only funny thing that had been said the whole morning. She gave him one to three years in the Nevada State prison system. If she had not had a laugh out of it, she might have given him six years. I was just happy that I would know where he was for at least a year or two.

CHAPTER 14

HIGH DESERT STATE PRISON

After the initial shock of visiting Michael at High Desert State Prison the first time, I tried to see him every week on Saturday. It was a long forty-five minute drive to the prison, but once I was accustomed to it, I would use it to spend time thinking and enjoying being alone.

My thoughts about my relationship with Michael were changing. To be honest, I really had had just about enough, and his incarceration was the final straw. I no longer thought about how I could help him. I could not, and frankly, never would be able to. It was not an understanding I came to easily. I had known it for some time, but with his incarceration, things became more concrete. The only person in the whole world who could change the direction Michael was going was Michael himself. Yes, I could provide background support, but I no longer thought of myself as a person who could influence him. It was as if I were a friend he could count on to be there, but not one who could, or would, save him from anything. It gave me the peace I had not had in a long, long time. And I knew where he was, and that he was safe. I slept a lot better after his incarceration than I did before it.

Still, it was not always easy for me to think about my son being in prison. One visit coincided with Michael's 28th birthday. In the last year, he had spent Thanksgiving, Christmas, and his birthday in prison. Not that birthdays and holidays were the most important things in life, but they are the times when families make memories and spend time together. As I sat in the waiting area and reflected on these milestones, I felt both sad and angry. After all, it was not just himself that he had hurt—it was his whole family. Moreover, as I looked around me, I realized that each of the families visiting had experienced the same disruptions in their lives. How many birthdays and holidays had been sacrificed because of our loved ones' problems? I don't think I could have counted them if I had tried. It was a sad testimony to the lives we all had endured.

Holidays and birthdays have never been good days for Michael. For most people they are something to look forward to and celebrate. For Michael, they were always something to dread. As I sat down and wished him a happy birthday, I saw his eyes narrow just a bit as he tilted his head to the side. I knew he was probably thinking about how he was spending his birthday again this year. He did not look happy to be twenty-eight and in prison.

He seemed changed after spending time in prison. I was not sure if it was for the better or not. Maybe it is just the way people change when they are incarcerated for long periods. They have to adapt, or otherwise they would go crazy.

He had begun using prison slang: "homey" or "homeboy" for *friend* and "celly" for *cellmate*. He was also stronger and fitter. There was not much to do there except work out. He did push-ups in the cell and made weights out of plastic bags filled with water. He told me he did one hundred push-ups and one hundred squats every morning and then ran three miles every night. On the weekends, he played handball or baseball.

It was freezing cold the next time I visited, just a month after his birthday. The ground in the High Desert area had a light blanket of sparkling snow covering the ground, shining like a sheet of ice. It was beautiful and serene, until you saw the ugliness of the buildings and fences. I vaguely wondered if the snow could possibly affect the electrical energy of the fence around the prison.

Indoors, everyone was sitting and chatting as if they were at home in their living rooms. Some of them played cards or dominos. Some ate junk food, but most just sat, heads down, holding hands and talking quietly. Occasionally someone got up and asked permission to take a photo with their family.

Prisons allow inmate photographers to take photos during visiting. The inmates assigned to photography have Polaroid cameras and will take your photo for a certain amount of earned credit or points. The guards call the photographer, and then the visitors who want the photo taken pose against a painted wall. Usually families can take the photos with them when they leave, but in some prisons, the photographer uses a digital camera and has to send the photos out for processing. In that case, the inmates mail them to their families later. We had photos taken several times. I kept them locked in a box and only looked at them on certain occasions—though never on a holiday or birthday, but usually the day after. Somehow it meant more to me then.

Visitors can stay as long as they want during visiting hours, unless the room is so crowded that the guards have to limit the visiting time. In the two years I visited Michael there, I never saw that happen. On any given day, there were about forty visitors, usually mothers, girlfriends, wives, and children. Most of the black and Hispanic prisoners had a lot of family members visiting, although few fathers of any color visited. The children were a problem for me. I was never able to decide whether it was a good thing or not. On the one hand, the kids get to see their parent. On the other hand, how good is it for them to pass through those steel gates, take the long walk up to the visitors' building, and then see their mom or dad come through yet another barred door? I did not know the answer, but I did wonder how many of them faced the same destiny as their parents.

All of these children now lived in a single-parent home. They were denied having a family that is whole, and they were learning firsthand about crime and its consequences. Would they learn from it, or would they learn about it? Would the propensity for crime be passed on from father or mother to son or daughter, or would it be the very thing that motivated them to do well in life?

After Michael went to prison, Jennifer and Danny came to stay with me for almost a year. I still heard from Erica and Sarah too, but they stayed in California and I only saw them infrequently. I debated for months whether to bring Danny to the prison. I was worried about the effect it would have on him. Finally I did bring him, and he seemed glad to see his father, but he only came with me a few times. The fact that he did not ask me to take him more often told me I was right not to force visits.

Danny and one of my brothers were the only people, besides me, to visit Michael the entire time he was there. Many prisoners never receive any visitors. The longer they are incarcerated, the fewer people remember them or come to see them. People get involved in their own lives, and those who are locked away from society may be forgotten. Sometimes it is a matter of the family even having the means to visit at all. Other times, it is just that the family members and loved ones have had enough and can't endure any more hurt. In some cases, some of the family members are illegal aliens and are afraid to chance being caught and possibly deported, so they never visit at all.

Not having visitors is the very worst thing for prisoners, because they lose their one real tie to the outside world. Incarceration cuts off prisoners from society and forces them to live in a stagnant world that does not change. Prisons do nothing to keep inmates integrated with the world; in fact, the world does not want to know about them. Most people would rather just see them warehoused away somewhere, where they will not be a bother to the general population. Cut off and isolated, inmates are not able to learn how to behave in society. They lose touch with what is going on. They may not know how to use a computer or smart phone. They may forget how to dress, or even how to order in a restaurant. Instead they learn how to act, look, and behave like criminals. Prisoners find themselves in a solitary, sad circumstance. I knew that my visits were keeping Michael tied to the real world, and I hoped it would help when the time came for his reentry to the outside.

CHAPTER 15

THE VISITING ROOM

The warden came by one afternoon while we were sitting in the visiting room. I am not sure why, but this was the second time I had seen him during that visit. Maybe he was just making his rounds. All the prisoners smiled and said hello, and then after he passed by, there was an undercurrent of murmuring which could be felt more than heard. Inmates make it their business to dislike the warden. They want to place the blame for their sorry circumstances somewhere besides on their own shoulders, where it belongs.

Michael said, "See that? He's just coming around to make us think there is something going down. That's just bullshit."

"Why would he do that? I think he has enough to do with all of you charming guys in here already."

Michael had just finished telling me why all the other inmates said they shouldn't be in prison. Some other guy did it, their lawyer screwed up, they were falsely accused, the jury didn't know what they were doing, the judge was prejudiced, it was mistaken identity, the DNA sample wasn't really theirs, the drug test was inaccurate, it was their money and not the other guy's, their father beat them, they came from the ghetto, etc., etc. Apparently, no one in the whole place was guilty except Michael. They had all been framed. What an amazing set of coincidences. I just laughed.

Michael also told me how inmates keep their scams and businesses going even on the inside. One inmate, he said, did alterations and made Hacky Sacks out of leftover material and unpopped popcorn. One guy did tattoos. He made his equipment from the motor of a CD player, a pen capsule, guitar strings from the chapel guitar, and ink from pens. He glued the pen capsule to the motor, which allowed it to go up and down. The ink flowed down the capsule to the guitar needle so the tattoo could be drawn. The result was a prison tat. You can easily recognize prison tattoos, because they are usually done in black ink, and the lines are less defined than professional tattoos.

The ingenuity of inmates is amazing. Too bad they never used all that talent and ingenuity for doing good things on the outside. Another inventive inmate, Michael told me, was making "pruno" from fruit, water, and sugar. He fermented it in a plastic bag stolen from housekeeping, and had to burp it every few hours to keep it from bursting the plastic bag. It was a toss-up whether they got high from it, or just got the runs. They were probably lucky they did not get food poisoning.

Some ran gambling games and some, sports betting. There were also inmates who provided drugs or sex for commissary goods or stamps. Stamps were the definitive currency in the prison. I wondered how much of it the guards really knew about, and how much they just let happen to keep the stability of the prison environment.

When I asked Michael if he was drug-free, he said, "Hell yes—you don't think I want to go down on one of those jerk-offs, do you?"

It had always been hard to tell when Michael was drug-free, except when he was really strung out and had lost a lot of weight. He had used so long that he had gotten good at hiding the effects. I was looking in his eyes and could not even tell that day.

"How do the drugs get smuggled in?"

"The guards bring some of it in, but mostly it's done right here in the visiting room right under the guard's nose. See that Chicano over there?" He looked to his right at a young, long-haired Hispanic man with what looked like his wife or girlfriend. He had gang tattoos on his neck and arms. She was so thin that she bordered on anorexic. Her skin was pale and her complexion bad, and she had tattoos on her arms too. Rings circled each of her fingers. Her nail polish was purple.

I looked over. "What about him?"

"When his little druggie girlfriend came in, she had a stash in her mouth. When he came in he was allowed one kiss, and that is when they made the transfer. Then he swallowed it, and three days from now he has his drugs. He puts a piece of plastic or something over the toilet to catch the stash, and there you go. Me, I don't want to dig through my shit even for drugs."

Drugs are everywhere on the yard and in the prison. It is incredible how easy it is to get drugs into penal institutions. I personally saw visitors abusing the rules and passing drugs when they thought they weren't being watched. I wondered how many of the inmates were even doing drugs while visiting, rather than trying to take them back to the cellblock.

After one of my visits, Michael called and told me they'd had him take a drug test after I left. I asked why and he replied, "They thought you passed me something when we were eating popcorn. Stupid idiots."

"That's ridiculous. I wouldn't do anything like that. Don't they know I'm your mother?"

"Yeah, they do, but do you know how many guys get stuff even from their mothers? I told them you were so straight you would not even look at drugs, never mind pass them. I said you would rather strangle me than pass drugs to me. Anyway, I don't have anything to worry about. I'm clean."

The next time I visited, I was more careful where I put my hands. I did not put them in my pockets, and I tried to keep them above the table. I looked at the cameras in the glass domes in the ceiling and made sure I didn't turn away from them. It was like a comedy; the more I tried to look innocent, the more I looked like I was doing something illegal. I was making such an effort not to appear suspicious, that the guards were probably singling me out to watch.

I felt guilty again, even though I had not done a thing. How was it that all this made me feel like a prisoner instead of a visitor? And it was not just me; I had heard the same comments from many of the other visitors as they were questioned, searched, and told where to stand and what to do. Many visitors had even been turned away for being a couple of minutes late, or had been intimidated during pat-downs. Once I had to take my underwire bra off so I could get in; fortunately, I had a sweater to cover up with, or I would have had to leave. The day before that incident, the guard had let me through even though the hand-held wand used for body searches had buzzed. She had just asked me if I had an underwire bra on, and let me go. I knew what the rules were for. I knew that the guards were trying to keep control over what was going on in the visiting area and behind the prison walls. However, at times like these I felt like I was being punished for what others did. I felt like the guards blamed me because my son was a criminal, and it seemed like they passed negative judgment on me and everything I had or had not done raising my son.

I was feeling out of sorts, so I tried to distract myself by asking Michael about the other inmates in the room. "So what's the older guy over there in for?" I asked trying not to make it obvious I was talking about a man four tables over, visiting with a young woman dressed in black slacks and a white shirt. I had spoken to her while we were waiting to get in to visit. We had talked about our mutual problems with the guards, and she had seemed educated and polite. I wondered who and why she was visiting.

"Oh, that's Pops. We call him that because he is one of the oldest cons here. He's here for murder one. That's his second wife he married while in here. He killed the first one. Yep, that's Pops all right. He will never see the light of day again. And see the sweet, innocent-looking kid over there?" Michael asked as he pointed to a clean-cut young man about twenty-five years old, with blond hair, blue eyes, and no tattoos.

I nodded.

"Well, he's here for murder one too. Killed someone while he was robbing a gas station. Of course he says it was a case of mistaken identity. Too bad the station had security cameras. You kinda can't deny it when your face is right there on the video, with the gun in your hand, shooting the clerk. And for what? A few measly hundred dollars?"

"Guess you never know just by looking," I replied, thinking the young man looked just like any other person on the street. And thinking, as I looked at my son, with his tattoos, Aryan Warrior insignia, and shaved head, that you really can't always tell by looks.

CHAPTER 16

MEDICAL CARE IN PRISON

Michael did not call often because the telephone companies charge an exorbitant rate for calls from prisons and jails. The only way to get phone calls for a reduced rate is to sign up with whichever company is offering deals for prison calls. Still, whenever he called between visits, I would press five to accept the call.

One day his voice sounded rough.

"What's wrong, Michael? You don't sound like you feel good." A mother always knows when her child is not well, even if they are in prison.

"I wasn't feeling so hot, and after five days of waiting and complaining they finally took me to medical. I've been running a fever, don't have any appetite, and am tired all the time. All my joints are aching, too. All I do is lie in bed and feel like crap.

"So, they finally got me to the nurse. She gave me some Tylenol—big damn deal—took some blood, and sent me on my merry way back to my cell. Then about a week later, she calls me back to medical and says I have hepatitis C. So I'm like, what's that mean? She tells me it is a virus which attacks your liver, and can be very serious. She said I probably got it from injecting drugs or getting tattoos. Either way, I have it."

"What are they going to do about it? Are they treating you for it?"

"No, not yet. She said to wait and see if I ride this out...Mom, I am really feeling terrible, and I don't think Tylenol is the cure."

I wasn't an expert on hepatitis, but I did know it could be dangerous. If left untreated, it could make him more prone to cirrhosis and carcinoma of the liver later in life. "You need to go back and tell her you want to see a doctor and be treated."

"According to her, the lab work says I don't have any liver damage, so it is a wait-and-see game. I saw one of my gang brothers take the treatment, and he was sicker with the treatment than with the hep C. He was laid up for weeks and got so thin it was ridiculous. So I think I will just wait and see if I pull through this."

I was not happy with this solution, but I didn't have any way to change it except by getting Michael to force the issue in the prison. "Look, I would rather you got the treatment, but if you won't, just keep me apprised of how you are. And if you get worse, please get the treatment."

The rate of hepatitis in the penal system is very high—according to William Cassidy at HCV Advocate, from 13 to 54 percent, depending on the facility.[2] It is extremely expensive to treat the disease. Due to prison budget constraints, medical personnel have to make decisions on whether to treat, based on the severity of the inmate's symptoms. This means medical care in prison can be very limited for the treatment of hepatitis C and other chronic diseases.

Finally Michael recovered enough so I could visit again. When I arrived, I gave the prison guard my son's name and waited. Sometimes it took a while for them to locate him, but that day it took ages. I sat alone at the table looking at the other visitors and prisoners, though with fugitive glances so I didn't interfere with their privacy. After about twenty-five minutes, I got up and asked for Michael again. I spoke to the female custodian, who had never said a civil word to me before and usually treated me like I was a prisoner too. I tried my usual tactic, which was to be overly nice, and for a change it worked. She called around for him, but he still wasn't to be found.

At first I thought it was really quite funny they couldn't find a prisoner. "How hard can it be?" I said, smiling. "He can't go that far."

2 William Cassidy, "Hepatitis C Infection in Prisons," *HCV Advocate: Medical Writer's Circle* (Sacramento, CA: Hepatitis C Support Project, 2003), http://www.hcvadvocate.org/hcsp%5Carticles/cassidy-1.html.

She, however, did not think it was funny at all, so I sat down, a scolded child. He was not in his cell and not in school. After about an hour with me sitting and wondering what was going on, she called me over and said she was still trying to locate him. I was getting very worried that he had had a relapse and was in the medical unit. I couldn't imagine what the problem was unless he was sick.

When they finally found him, I had been sitting for an hour and a half.

"Where were you?" I asked. By now I was practically frantic and my voice trembled with worry.

"I was in the coffee shop on a break from school," he said after our allowed one kiss and hug. "I had some gambling debts to collect. I won twelve stamps, six packages of soup, and a pack of coffee playing pinochle last night."

"Well, I've been sitting here almost an hour and a half. You need to be where they can find you when I'm coming. It is a waste of my time to just sit here." I was still upset, because I had been worried that he was still sick or that something serious had happened.

We talked a little about his medical care, or lack thereof. He told me that the doctor only came once a week, and the rest of the time they saw a nurse or a nurse practitioner. If one of the inmates was critically sick, they would be transported to a hospital, where they would get the same care everyone else does. I was just glad he was feeling better, even though he looked pale and thin.

Seeing I was still upset Michael tried to change the mood of the conversation by using humor. "It's grazing time," he said, watching everyone at the vending machines. "Did you ever notice how all the fat chicks and dudes eat all the stuff that's bad for you? Look at that one. Man, she looks like the high side of a Mack truck. I wouldn't want to get on her bad list."

"Give it a rest," I said. I was trying to keep my composure, but I was still on edge. I have always hated it when he says rude things about others. "You're not the prettiest guy on the block either." Now he knew he had my attention and kept it up.

"Look at that white chick over there. She looks like she has not slept in a month of Sundays. She must be on a meth high."

I looked, and the girl did look tired and worn out. Turning back to him, I said, "Yeah, but look who is looking at her." That shut him up for the moment. I knew he was just doing this to be funny, but I have always felt that underneath his comedy routines was something else. People who feel insecure put others down so they can feel better about themselves. It might be deeply hidden in his psyche, and he may not even realize it, but that's where I think it comes from. Maybe I am wrong, but then maybe I am not. As a rule most of his humor had usually been self-deprecating or just regular old funny jokes. He has never used crude or dirty humor, at least not around me.

I changed the subject and asked about school.

"It's going good, Mom. I have a lot of credits, and now that I have my GED I can take college courses. I think I would like to take creative writing." Michael has always loved to read, so this didn't surprise me.

"Maybe you should write about your experiences in prison. Quite a few inmates have written books about their lives. Maybe you could do some good with it. You know you used to speak at AA meetings all the time, and you were good at it."

He said he would think about it. "One thing I know for sure is that I could scare a few young people. They have a program in here where they bring young offenders from juvenile hall in, and some of the inmates tell them how it is. I think I would like to do that."

"Why don't you ask about doing it, then?"

Michael paused, shuffled his feet, and looked down at them. "I guess...I do look the part now with my shaved head and all my Aryan Warrior gang tattoos. I ought to be able to help someone. You know I've always had a burning desire inside me to help others. Remember when I wrote that *Death to Meth* program and put it on the Internet?"

"I remember that. It was a good program. However, I also know that most of the time your desire to help others has gotten you in trouble. Here's your chance to do something positive that won't get you in trouble."

A shadow crossed his face, and I knew he doubted himself. Self-doubt had sometimes been an issue for Michael; I think it held him back from achieving some of his goals and dreams. As I looked at him that day, I remembered all the times he could not sleep the night before starting a new year in school, or before beginning a new job. He would worry himself into a frenzy. Sometimes it seemed like the heavy chains of doubt would drown him in failure before he even started. He would then cover his feelings up with bravado.

I ended the visit by telling him he should be sure to request to be part of the program, and that he would be good at it. He gave me a long hug, and I walked out of the visitors' room with trepidation but with hope that he would carry out his plan. I knew it would benefit him in the end.

CHAPTER 17

ARYAN WARRIOR PRISON GANG

Races divide prisons. Although inmates appear to be civil to each other in the visiting area, there are divisions which inmates do not cross inside the steel double doors. When he first entered High Desert State Prison, Michael had been recruited by the Aryan Warriors (AW) to join their white supremacist gang. He was a prime target for them; he was white, had associated with skinheads in his youth, and was young and strong.

I thought he had outgrown his inclination toward that type of affiliation. He had admitted his alliance with the skinheads had been in defiance of us and in particular of his Jewish stepfather. At the time he had wanted to deeply hurt and offend us, which he accomplished. He had no idea of the history of white supremacists and the unspeakable crimes that had been committed in the name of their doctrine. Now, even though he did know their doctrine, he said he'd had to join something in order to survive within the walls of the prison.

On that first visit I had reminded him that through the years he'd had many friends of different races and religions, and had held no prejudice against them.

"Mom, you don't understand. In prison you have to hook up with someone or you will be killed or raped. There are four groups, the Hispanics, the blacks, the Asians, and the whites, although we don't have too many Asians in Nevada. I joined up with the AWs to have someone who would have my back when I wasn't looking. If it weren't for the gangs policing their own, the prisons would be a lot worse than they are.

Mostly the guards just sit back and let us mind our own house. That is, except for when they are taking bribes and helping us, and there is a lot of that. You have no idea."

I felt I needed to know about the gang and researched their origins. What I found out horrified me. As time would go on, I would find out even more about how they were organized and how they conducted their operations. There are approximately eight thousand Aryan Warrior members in the state of Nevada alone, and there are probably members of similar groups in every state of the nation. The motto of the Aryan Warriors is that white blood is pure, and they want to keep it that way. It is not clear to me whether they hate other races or just think they are superior.

They have a military-style hierarchy with a supreme horn holder as leader, a level of horn holders as secondary leaders and lieutenants, commanders, soldiers, and prospects rounding out the ladder of command. The leaders, who make decisions about who does what, are called "shot callers." The gang is well organized and communicates from facility to facility and from inside prisons to the outside. They use notes, codes, and word of mouth, along with messages and mail transported by friends and visitors. There isn't anywhere a gang member can't communicate to, even when they are in solitary confinement. They deal drugs in the prison and on the outside. Gambling and extortion are just a few of their other "businesses." Most people would never dream their influence was so far reaching and had such control in the prisons and in the community.

Most of the gang members are dangerous and must commit some type of violence in order to gain prestige within the gang. They are known for their ruthlessness, violence, and the penalties anyone pays, even one of their own, who crosses them or snitches. Even when you get out of prison, the Aryan Warriors expect you to continue your duties on the outside and provide funds from illegal dealings to gang members still in prison. Usually the only way you get out of the Aryan Warriors is in a body bag. Occasionally, if you get old enough and you have done enough for them, they will allow you to "retire."

By now, my son was at least a midlevel member of the gang. I did not know what he had to do to get to this level. I hoped he had not committed an act of violence, but I had my doubts. I was angry and upset. I hated the idea of what he was doing but did not have enough information to fight with him about it. What could I do other than desert or disown him? I guess some people would have said yes, I should absolutely disown him. But I could not. I may not have liked what he was doing, and I may have even hated it, but he was still my son. I was not able to, nor did I want to remove myself from that position.

It seemed if you did not belong to a gang, you were doomed, and if you did, you were doomed. Either way created problems which an inmate would have to deal with. If Michael tried to leave or cross them, they would target him to be hurt or killed in prison. He had taken a course for which I did not see any way out, at least until he was out of prison. Even then, they might still try to have a hold on him.

I felt the path he had taken would only serve to get him in some kind of trouble, and eventually it did.

One day Michael called and told me he was in trouble for being involved in a short-lived gang war and would be going to solitary confinement. I asked why he participated, and his answer was that he had to because he was in the gang that was involved in the war. If something happens on the yard, he told me, you have to be there to help your "brothers."

This is really stupid, I thought, but I tried to keep my tongue in my mouth. What good could my objections do? He already knew the difference between right and wrong, and if he chose to take a particular path, he only got what he should have expected.

He had no problem with this and even agreed. As an adult, he had never shied away from responsibility for his actions. I have always been grateful that he had taken this attitude and had accepted the consequences, but on the other hand, it was frustrating that the understanding he possessed had not convinced him to change.

The administration sent him to the Special Housing Unit (SHU) with about thirty others. Those who end up there refer to it as the "hole."

"I'll be transferred to a cell alone and won't have the use of any of my electronics. I won't be allowed into the yard and will only get a shower every three days. They will let me out one hour a day for exercise in a caged area. I'll probably be limited to a jump suit or my boxer shorts, and what they call 'nutritional meals' will be taken in the cell. The nutritional meals taste like paper, so I'm not looking forward to that. The regular prison food is bad enough."

While he was in the SHU, I was not able to visit for thirty days. It was the longest time I had not seen him since I began visiting. In a way, it was a relief. I wanted to see him, but each time I left the prison, it was depressing for me. I always felt dirty somehow. I just wanted to be treated a little more like a visitor than a criminal or parental failure. It seemed like the guards would look at me with disdain and detachment, as if I were just some animal to be herded down the corridor. Was it my own projection I was living with, or was it really that way? Sometimes I wondered. I was glad not to have to go, but then felt guilty that I was glad about it. My emotions were caught in a wringer that tired me out as if I had been up running for days.

After four weeks, Michael was out of the SHU. Things were quiet on the yard and there weren't any lockdowns at the facility for a while. Then there was a crisis for prison space, and the authorities transferred Michael to Ely State Prison. He made phone call after phone call asking me to do something to get him out of there. Ely, he said, was like a maximum-security prison. There were a lot of lifers there who did not care what happened to them, so they had nothing to lose. This bred a lot of violence. What could I do? Nothing! Luckily he only spent a few months there and then miraculously, or maybe by some clerical error, they transferred him to a step-down camp nearby.

The camp consisted of a set of long, low buildings similar to barracks, and was surrounded only by a chain-link fence. No towers, no razor wire, no guns, and no big deal to get into the visitors' room. What a relief for both of us! At the camp, they allowed the inmates a lot of freedom. It was a designated firefighting camp, part of the program the

State of Nevada runs to train inmates to fight forest fires, and they could earn the trust of the correctional officers.

"Michael, it looks like you lucked out this time. This place is like a ranch and is in an absolutely beautiful setting."

"I am going to take advantage of it. They even have a program for maintenance engineering, and I am going to join the program so I can learn to do something worthwhile."

By now Michael was almost thirty years old, and I was thinking to myself, it was about time. But I did not say it aloud. I knew he knew what I was thinking; I never could hide my feelings. I wore them like cloth of colors on my face.

We talked about the fact that some people with conduct disorder eventually mature around thirty years old and begin to live a normal life. We didn't talk about the fact that those who don't change usually spend the rest of their days in prison.

It was a good visit. He had grown his hair out and looked relatively normal. I could see he was doing well there. One female officer was partial to him and allowed me to stay a few minutes past visiting, because I had come so far.

I knew the road ahead was going to be difficult, but I left with high hopes that I could have my son back. The drive home to Las Vegas was filled with little things that added to my happiness: a golden, glowing sunset, a smooth drive home, and a flock of birds passing by in their migration south. The outdoors, which had often been my salvation, soothed my soul.

CHAPTER 18

THE SAME PROBLEMS

That visit was especially memorable because I was surprised to see a friend of mine visiting her son too that day. We ran into each other in the central parking lot prior to going in to visit. Her son was in the main prison. I had known Susan for many years through her parents, but had not realized she shared the same problems I had. After our visit, we met at a restaurant back in Las Vegas to compare notes.

It always helps if you have someone you can talk with. Her son, Matthew, was younger than Michael was and had been in prison just a few months. He had spent two months in the "fish tank" and now was in a twenty-three-hour-a-day lockup unit. The fish tank is where the guards keep all new prisoners when they first enter prison, so they can be observed twenty-four hours a day. It is a large dormitory with rows of beds in the open, and a separate area with tables and chairs meant for recreation.

"Julie, you can't imagine how horrible this has been. When they first sent Matthew here, I was so afraid for him because he was small. He had been doing drugs and he was very thin, too. I could just imagine what might happen to him, and I lay awake at night worrying about him. I don't even know how or why he got into drugs. I always thought he was a good kid. I never dreamed he would end up in prison."

She told me Matthew's troubles had started when he was just fourteen, right after his father died. He had begun taking OxyContin and Vicodin, and then, because the pills were so expensive and difficult to get, he moved on to heroin. Then he got a couple of DUIs. When he got the last one, the police found drugs in his car and sent him to jail.

Who knows why someone becomes addicted? How do they end it? I sure hadn't been able to figure it out. I'd had many of the same experiences with Michael. I could not count the sleepless nights I had spent worrying and wondering what had happened. It had always seemed so incongruous to me that anyone would want to ruin their life, hurt their loved ones, and throw their future away.

We sat drinking coffee while she talked for several hours. Trying to help Matthew had wiped her out emotionally and financially. She had sent him to a detox rehabilitation center, paid attorney's fees, paid fines, and paid for Suboxone programs to treat his need for heroin. She had lost many friends and had argued with family members who did not understand the problems she was having. Her Internet business had failed, even though it had been going well; she could not keep up with anything, and had put most of her business on the back burner. "It took all my strength and energy just trying to save his life," she said. "I barely slept. Always worrying I would go into his room and find him dead. It was happening to other friends of mine, and I knew it could happen to me too.

"Then he did overdose one evening while I was downstairs making dinner. One of his best friends called me and said to go check on Matthew right now because he had just talked to him and was worried about him being super-high. I went upstairs and found him blue. The friend had actually been with him, getting high on heroin, but had run next door so he wouldn't get in trouble. He called me because he did want to save Matthew's life. If he had not, Matthew would have died. That friend was a very sweet kid, with a lot of promise and a great family. He overdosed last year on heroin and died in his own parents' home."

I was overwhelmed by the depth of Susan's sorrow. I had been through most of these kinds of experiences myself, but it was heartrending to hear a friend tell the same sad story.

"You really find out who is toxic in your life and who truly supports you," she said, wiping her tears away. "I lost a lot of friends and family over this. My best friend finally said she did not want to associate with me anymore. She was tired of all the depression she saw in me, and how I always had Matthew on my mind. It is as if I am in prison too, right along with Matthew. People have blamed me, saying I was too lenient with him. Like I don't already blame myself every single minute. What mother wouldn't? Was it something I did raising him that could have caused this? Did I not tell him *no* enough? Was it because I was a single parent? Did I not handle his addiction problems right away? It's torn me apart. I don't need people judging how I raised Matthew or how I dealt with his addiction. I am already my biggest critic."

I said, "I know it is hard. I did have my family's support, but not my husband's, and I really could not blame him after all the things Michael did to him. Their support helped me get through it all. My brother even visited him, and he always called to see if I needed anything. I think I am lucky. Most of the people I have met during visiting have told me their families don't understand why they don't just give up on their loved ones who have gone to jail or prison"

As she pulled her feet up into the chair, Susan said, "My friends told me to throw him out because I was an enabler. Well, that may be true in some cases, but every situation and person is different. Some addicts do have to hit rock bottom. With other addicts, rock bottom is death, and that is where I thought Matthew would end up...dead. I knew him better than anyone else, and I knew he would be dead within a month if I threw him out. His only chance was with me."

She lifted her cup of coffee, then set it down. "They even asked me if I was mad at him. Had I told him that? Well, yes...I've said everything anyone could possibly think of and more. I've yelled, I've slapped his face, I've had thousands of hours of heart-to-heart talks with him. I've broken down to my lowest point and sobbed while I was begging him to stop the drugs. There's nothing I didn't express to him, or try." She looked off in the distance, paused, and continued. "No one was there in my shoes to see my life at home, and all they did was judge me needlessly. What I really needed was love and support."

Tears began to run down my face as I listened. How many other families and loved ones were on the outside, feeling the same way? Having the same problems? They feel isolated and cut off from everyone. They may be ashamed, as I was, and hide the fact that their loved one is in prison. They are too afraid to reach out to others, even those who could offer assistance. Sometimes they think that getting help would be impossible and that no one would listen to them. They may not even have a family or church to turn to. They aren't aware that there are organizations that will help, that will listen, and that will not judge them because of their loved ones' crimes.

Others do not always understand, even when drug addiction or mental illness lead to someone being incarcerated. All they see is a drug addict or a criminal, not a human being. I have even had people, not knowing my son was in prison, say things like "They should just shoot them all and be done with it." They even refer to them as animals. It is so hurtful, and perpetuates the shame that the family and loved ones of the inmates feel.

There are support groups out there, and some of them are online. The easiest to access are the various prison information websites and forums for families and friends of inmates. Members not only discuss their problems, but will also help with information when they can. Some members are former inmates who want to help. If a prison is on lockdown, someone will write about it. If a phone company is offering deals for calls from prisons, you will find information about it there. If you just need to talk, you will find someone who will fill that need.

Some users post questions, like the mother who went to visit her son to find out he had been beaten black and blue, his eyes bloody red. He almost refused her visit because he did not want her to see him. She found out that if he complained or told the guards who beat him up, he would be marked for even greater abuse. It made it easier for her to understand why he did not want to see her. When I heard about things like this I understood a little better why Michael had joined the Aryan Warriors.

There are also heartbreaking stories of parents who have mortgaged their homes and used their retirement funds to pay for attorneys. There are wives and girlfriends who don't know how they will survive alone, and families who end up in debt because they can't support themselves on one income. There are moms who take the children to school and then have to go to their jobs, and grandparents who move in to help the family. And then there are the children who cry themselves to sleep at night because they miss their mother or father.

Saddest of all are the stories about the failures: how a loved one who was released returned to the life they led before, and ended up back in prison a second or third time. Their families have to endure seeing their hopes shattered once again. Unfortunately, many ex-felons are not rehabilitated, and do not learn from the prison experience. It is hard to understand the motivation that drives young men and women to return to the same kind of life they were living before. What is it? Drugs? Low self-esteem? Poverty? Lack of support? I'm not sure anyone knows the entire answer. I do know it affects not only the person in prison, but the inmate's loved ones as well.

There are no bars or gates separating the pain and heartache from the inmates' families. Most devastatingly, the children suffer severely from not having that parent with them or their love to help them through life. The inmates write in their letters how much they miss their children, but it's no comparison to children who cry themselves to sleep at night or have to explain to friends or teachers why their mommy or daddy is in prison. How are children supposed to cope with that? What are they to say when another child teases them? There are no perfect answers, but there are support systems out there.

"That's been my life," said Susan. "But I am planning to give Matthew the tools to succeed when he gets out. I want him to be able to go to university and find a way back to life. No matter what happens, he is still my son and I will love him and stand by him until I die. And we are closer than ever because of all of this. I just want him to know I am here to support him."

As terrible as all this was, we finally found something to laugh about. We both said Amazon was our savior. Any little thing helps when someone is incarcerated, and we had both used Amazon to send books to our sons so they could have something concrete from the outside. You want them to have something, anything, even if it is just a book to hang on to.

CHAPTER 19

COMING HOME

The wait for Michael to get out of camp and start parole was only a couple of months, but seemed like forever. I drove to Ely to pick him up, and we were both very positive about how the rest of his life was going to be. His hair had grown out, and although he had a lot of tattoos, most of them could be hidden with clothing. He looked like any normal young person you might meet on the street. As a benefit from being in prison so long, he no longer smoked.

The first stop the next day was the parole office. His parole officer was a big black man with muscles that stood out beneath his shirt, and a neck as thick as a bull's. It was obvious he used his bulk to intimidate his charges. His olive-green eyes seemed to look inside you. He told Michael the rules and what he expected of him, and then he sent him directly into the restroom for a urine drug test. I could see there would be no fooling around with him, and I was glad of it.

Even Michael knew he had better toe the line or he would be right back where he started from, or worse. He was to report on a weekly basis, get a job, and show the officer his payroll stubs after he landed the job. He would be subject to random drug testing, even at home, and would have weekly parole visits for the first three months. If he did well, the visit schedule would be relaxed.

Michael had nowhere to live, and because I was no longer married, I let him live with me until he could get his own place. I did have an ulterior motive. I figured that if he was right there, I could keep an eye on what he was doing. Not that I could do anything about it, but I would have a better chance of knowing if he was screwing up again.

The first few days he was quiet. He seemed almost stunned by things on the outside: the number of people, the noise, the fast food, and the way everyone dressed. He stayed close to home for almost a week. Even after that, he seemed reticent to do anything alone. He even asked permission to use the bathroom. I thought this was a good thing. Maybe seeing how different it was to live on the outside would give him the incentive to stay out of prison forever and follow the rules.

When he finally seemed comfortable with life outside of prison, I bought him a cheap pickup truck so he could get around and find a job. He made a promise he would pay me back when he could.

It took him weeks to find a job. At first I thought he was not putting the effort into job hunting I felt he should be, but then I suspected the problem was that he had to document his felony conviction on applications. The average citizen has no idea how difficult it is to get a job when you have to answer yes to the question on the job application "Do you have any felony convictions?" As soon as the hiring managers saw this, they would just say, "We will take your application into consideration." He would never hear from them again. How can a person succeed when they cannot get a job?

Then somehow he did find a job. It actually was a good position with a local landscaping company that wanted him to start right away. They knew about his felony conviction, but thought he was a person they could take a chance on.

The chance they took worked out for both him and the company. He would come home and talk about how proud he was of himself to be doing a job like he was. He even got a raise, which we celebrated by going to our favorite Mexican restaurant for chicken tacos. He worked hard, and eventually they gave him a truck to drive and made him a supervisor.

Eight months later he asked me to help him buy a house. Of course he did not have any credit or down payment.

"Mom, I need a place of my own. I can pay for it. I just need a little help to get started. I promise you I will pay the mortgage and keep my job."

I was reluctant because of the last experience, but eventually I took money from my 401(k) plan and put a down payment on a small house. I thought that because the housing market in Las Vegas was booming, I couldn't lose, even if he left or lost his job. We found used furniture and got him the basics. I was happy for him. I was sure he would be able to maintain, particularly now that he had a place of his own and had been doing well with his job for close to a year. The future looked positive.

I was busy cleaning my house one day when he came by to talk. He had been in his own house for about six months.

"My boss gave me some extra paperwork at the job, and I goofed up. I really didn't know how to do it, and I did not want them to know, so I faked it and it wasn't right. So now they are putting me on probation, demoting me, and sending me to their Reno office. I have to drive up there tomorrow."

My heart skipped a beat and my hands trembled. Now that there had been a first failure, I was worried it would lead to more. It seemed once he had a disappointment, it always led to more problems, and he would begin to feel desperate. Then he would just spiral out of control.

The next night he called to tell me he had been in an accident on his way to Reno. Of course he had damaged the company truck, and as a result, he lost his job. At that time I just took it as bad luck. Or had he been on drugs? Later I learned that he had been nervous, had stayed up all night and then had driven when he was too tired. Eventually I found out he had been drinking energy drinks from the truck stop to stay awake, but had been too tired for them to work. He should have just pulled over. The only good part was that no one had been hurt, including him.

After that, there was another job hunt. He finally found a job laying block with a company he had worked for before. Unfortunately, one of the owner's sons was a former druggie friend of his, and then the problems really started. It wasn't long before he began missing work or showing up late constantly. They fired him. All I could do was wait for his eventual failure—and maybe even jail time again.

Now when I drove by his house, there would be strange people there. Our arguments began again—the same arguments we'd had years ago, when he was in the first house. It seemed like déjà vu, arguing about drugs, money, and the fact that he wasn't working.

"The house is in my name, and it is getting trashed. Either get rid of these people or everyone leaves, including you." I was no longer afraid of him being out on the street. He was old enough to take care of himself.

"Yeah, yeah, they will be gone in the morning."

Of course they weren't. I was so tired of the arguments and the stress that I could hardly bring myself to think about it, so I stayed away for a while. I was so disappointed that he was heading down the same path as before. It made me feel tired and old.

Then all of a sudden, the bills were paid and he had money to buy things. Whenever I went to visit, the house was clean. There was always some girl there, cleaning up. There were too many electronic toys around: new TVs with large screens, cell phones, stereos, and small, fancy motorbikes. You have to have money to buy those kinds of things.

I knew this was not good. "What are you doing to get this money, since you aren't working?"

"Nothing illegal like you think, Mom. I'm just doing a few favors for other people."

He insisted everything was fine, but I had a bad feeling. I would meet him at his house or in nearby restaurants to try to find out what was going on. I was also worried because the house was in my name, and it could be a liability for me. I knew something was wrong, but I could not prove a thing.

CHAPTER 20

FBI ARREST AND INCARCERATION

Months went by before it all finally ended. Michael called from the Clark County Detention Center. The police had picked him up and taken him to jail. He asked if I would bail him out, and I said I would not. Not this time or ever. He had been headed this direction for some time, and his own actions had led to this.

We had both seen it coming. Just two weeks before they caught him, I had met him at a pizza place in a nearby strip mall. He said he just wanted to see me; he did not have any motive other than just to visit and talk. I saw he had parked quite a distance from the restaurant, which I thought was strange. When I got inside, I found him sitting in the front area, watching the door. I had no idea what might be going on.

Then Michael started talking. "Mom, I'm being followed right now, and I am scared. Someone, the police or the FBI, has been sitting outside my house for a week. See the car out there? The silver Ford sedan? Well, it's an undercover FBI car, and they are definitely on my tail. Those two guys sitting in the car will come in here. You just wait and see."

Drugs had made him paranoid in the past, and that was what I thought was wrong this time. He didn't seem to have any other signs of drug use, though; he was eating, and his eyes were not dilated. However, it was difficult for me to believe for a minute that the FBI would be interested in him. And what would it be for? If it was drugs, it should be the police who were after him, not the FBI.

We started eating our lunch, and sure enough, the two men from the Ford came in. They were in their late twenties or early thirties, wearing Dockers and button-down shirts. I noticed they also had military haircuts. To me they looked like engineers, but there was something different about them. They were extremely fit, and they did seem to keep glancing at us. Eventually they took a seat in the back, but at a table where they could watch us.

Michael was tapping his foot, like he always did when he was nervous. The more nervous he got, the faster the foot went. I began to feel a little scared myself. What if they decided to do something right there in the middle of the restaurant?

After we finished eating, Michael seemed to want to talk some more. Not about anything special, just to chat—almost as if he thought he might not see me for a long time. That ended up being true.

The two men left, but as they passed by, they seemed to look right at us. I wasn't sure if they knew who I was or not.

Michael said, "See, I told you so."

I still wasn't certain. "You don't know that for sure. And even if they are FBI, what would they want with you?"

"You don't want to know."

The Ford drove away from the restaurant, but only to the other side of the parking lot.

When we were finished with lunch, Michael walked me to my car. I sat there a few minutes and waited for him to leave. The Ford followed him out of the parking lot. Now I was paranoid myself, but what could I do? I couldn't change him or his life; only he could do that, and clearly he had not. I knew he was in for a terrible time shortly. I just hoped he didn't get shot. Getting arrested would be bad enough.

Days turned into weeks before I heard from him again. Finally the police caught up with him. When they pulled him over he tried to get away, and when they caught him they searched the car for probable cause. They found a small amount of drugs, drug paraphernalia, and a stolen gun. That is when I got the call I had been dreading.

It is surprising how small a thing can trip someone up who is wanted by the police. I found out the police had stopped Michael because of a faulty taillight. The police had indeed been following him, and had been waiting for an opportunity to stop him.

Wouldn't you think that if you were trying to avoid the police, you would make sure everything on your vehicle was in accordance with the law? So many criminals are caught this way. It is incredible how stupid they can be.

The gun had been registered in California, and he had gotten it from someone who had brought it across the state line. This would become an important point, because it was considered organized interstate trafficking of weapons, which was a RICO offense. RICO is the Racketeer Influenced and Corrupt Organization Act, enacted in order to allow extended penalties for convictions of organized criminal acts. It meant that Michael now would qualify for the extended punishment. This put him in a very bad position as far as how sentencing would go.

After several days, Michael was moved to the North Las Vegas Detention Center. It was an impressive complex, with a huge, domed front building for the North Las Vegas court and a long side building that housed the visitors' center. Behind them was a block building with razor wire around it and tiny windows way up high on the third floor. Michael would end up spending over three years there, most of it in solitary confinement, awaiting trial.

On my first visit I walked into the entrance area, which had a metal detector that was not working and a small window where you could go to speak to the officer on duty. There was also a hall which led around the corner to the lockers and the restrooms. It was not like High Desert Prison at all, where there were high-tech metal detectors and guards sitting at a desk in the large waiting area. Compared with the rest of the building, this section seemed like it was built almost as an afterthought.

I was familiar with the drill now and was not so paranoid, but was just as upset as I was the first day I visited Michael at High Desert State Prison. This time, at least, I wasn't crying. I walked up to the check-in window and asked what I needed to do to visit. I already knew they only allowed visits once a month for thirty minutes. The visiting hours at High Desert had been every Friday evening, and on Saturdays and Sundays, all morning and most of the afternoon.

The clerk was surly. "Just wait out there. You'll be called by the guard."

Great, I thought, I am going to be treated like a criminal again. Why was it that they seemed to always act that way? It felt exactly the same as before, and I had hoped it might be different this time, but it was not. Right on the hour, the guard showed up and escorted the few of us who were there into the visiting area. It was located behind locked doors and had three rows of long tables, with phones and monitors at each station. It was not until then that I realized we were not going to be able to visit in person, only by television monitor. This was a no-contact facility. I would not be able to give him a hug or even touch his hand for the next three years.

After waiting about five minutes, I saw Michael coming on the monitor. He was in an ill-fitting orange jumpsuit, and his feet were shackled. His hands were shackled to a leather belt around his waist, so tightly that he had a hard time picking up the phone. He grasped the phone with both hands and raised it to his ear, elbows tight to his body. I was overcome. There on the monitor was a real criminal. I had never seen Michael like this before.

He had not lost all of his charm, though. "Hi Mom. It's great to see you looking so good. Thanks for coming."

I was holding back tears. "It's good to see you too, but why in the world do they have you chained up like this?"

He looked down, and all I could see on the monitor was the top of his forehead and his newly shaved head. "They think I'm dangerous because of my membership in the Aryan Warriors."

I sat there, not really knowing what to say.

"Mom, you know yourself that in prison you have to belong to a gang. I have people to protect my back, and there are things I need to do. Those are the rules you have to live by."

Until that time, I had not truly understood the hold they keep on their members. Michael explained that all members must contribute to the "cause" even when they get out of prison. In fact, the reason Michael had been under surveillance by the police and the FBI was for suspicion of selling drugs and providing funds to Aryan Warriors still in prison. His affiliation with the Aryan Warriors had been his downfall.

"So what has all that to do with this arrest and your head being shaved again?"

The explanation spun out like an incredible crime story. "You might as well know, right now I am being charged by the Feds with a lot of things that add up to more RICO charges. The district attorney charged me with transportation of a stolen weapon across state lines, selling methamphetamine, forging fake IDs, selling stolen goods, and some other stuff. In addition, they are charging me, and the rest of the Aryan Warrior members they have rounded up in here, with stuff that happened at Ely State Prison. One of the gang members stabbed another one, and eventually the dude died. There was also extortion, gambling, and illegal relationships with the guards, who were helping us bring in and distribute drugs in prison. Although the district attorney is charging me with almost all of this shit, I had mostly just participated in the gambling and organization of the drugs, but they don't really care about who did what as long as you are a member of the gang. I was not even in Ely State Prison when all the bad shit went down. That was the time when the guy got stabbed and all. The problem is, as a member of the gang, I am associated with them and the charges." He rocked back in the plastic chair.

Now the house of cards I had been propping up for so many years came tumbling down. I was sure I would faint, but I didn't. I thought I would cry, but couldn't even do that. My son was a career criminal.

We both just sat there, not speaking, the gravity of it all hanging like a weight between us.

After I left I was not sure I could drive home, so I went to the McDonald's next door to get a cup of coffee. I did not really see or talk to anyone...just sat there by myself. The restaurant was busy, people lined up at the counter to order, but I did not even notice them. There was not one clear thought in my head. Finally I pulled myself together and left. I knew I had done everything I could, and still nothing had worked this time, or any other time before. It always just fell apart, no matter what I had hoped for. Frustrated and angry, I pulled out my Serenity Prayer from the glove compartment of my car. I read the prayer for the hundredth time, and drove away.

—w—

God grant me the serenity
To accept the things I cannot change;
Courage to change the things I can;
And the wisdom to know the difference.
—Reinhold Niebuhr

—w—

CHAPTER 21

RICO TRIAL

The month went by, and the next visit I arrived with a list of questions. What was going to happen? When would he go to trial? Who was his attorney? What did he think the penalties would be? Would they put him in a federal prison out of state?

I had gone back and forth over whether to visit anymore. Should I continue to support someone who never changed and was now a career criminal? It is difficult to explain how I felt. Many people would not even think twice of walking away for good. I knew that, and could not blame them for those feelings. However, it is easy to say you would not, when it is not your son, daughter or loved one. I had a lot of conflict over the decision. I was ashamed and angry, and sometimes I felt that maybe I did not want to continue visiting—that maybe I was too tired of it all, and it was too ardous and demanding on my soul. I also thought about all his good qualities, his love for his family, his sense of humor, and his caring and thoughtful side. In the end, he was still my son and I loved him, so I visited. Unless he killed someone, I would stand by him with my moral support.

I was his mother and I could not change that, no matter what. Somehow you just can't get away from that. I know I could not. I did hear of parents who disowned their children, but for the most part the parents seemed loyal. The wives and girlfriends were a different story. They were often not able to stay true. It is challenging to carry on the responsibilities of a family alone, and without any kind of monetary support, they sometimes drifted away for better opportunities. The future was clouded with potential problems, and money was usually short. If they were young, they wanted to have a complete life, not wait for someone who might not get out for a long time.

Many family members struggled the same way I did. One family member I met during that second visit to the North Las Vegas Detention Center was a young Hispanic girl with three children. She was a legal alien with a green card, and was holding down a receptionist job while she took care of the children. She had all three of her children with her that day so they could visit their dad. They hung on to her skirt or played quietly while they waited to be let in. She sat next to me, talking about how tough her life was now and how much she felt her children were suffering.

Her husband was in the same unit as Michael, but of course was not one of the Aryan Warriors. They had charged him with burglary and forgery, and he was awaiting trial. She said she did not know what had happened to him, because he had been a different person when she had married him. Once he lost his job, he had turned to friends who were running illegal schemes. They forged credit cards and then used them to order expensive appliances and other items online. Then they would have the items delivered to empty houses where they would pick them up. They were also selling fake ID cards and fake credit cards.

She was struggling with the fact that her husband might not be home for a long time. How was she to manage on her own? She had loved him, but now wondered if she should stay married to a criminal or try to make a life for herself and her children without him. Of course he said he would change, but how was she to know if he would? Moreover, what would happen if she waited five or ten years, and then he did not change? Even her parents were encouraging her to give up on him.

Her sorrow and pain were evident in the way she talked about her husband and the sad smile on her face when she looked for some small support from a stranger. As she gathered her children to her to prepare to enter the visiting area, I wished I could tell her what to do, but how could I take away her one bit of hope? I had also experienced the continual regret and feeling of hopelessness that comes from being disappointed repeatedly. How could I tell her it would be okay when I did not really feel like it would? She needed to take care of herself and her children, and secretly I hoped she would give him up and move on with her life. There was so much more out there for her and her children.

I was still thinking about the young girl and her children when I went in to visit with Michael. It was making me feel angry and frustrated with him. When he told me, "I guess you don't really understand what I had to do," I said to him, "I guess I don't. But it seems the people you were associating with only got you in more trouble. Now you are back in prison and indicted in a federal trial. How did that work out for you?"

It may have sounded mean, but that is how I was feeling. "You and only you are making these choices. That's the way it has been for a long time. You know right from wrong, and you have always been taught values. You are not some stupid, ignorant person. How can you keep making these terrible choices that land you back in prison?"

"I don't know," he said. "I just fall back into where I am comfortable, and I feel like I am helping out people who need me."

"Well, how about the fact that I need you too. What about that? Where will you be this Christmas and next year on everyone's birthday? Where will you be when your children need you? Tell me that."

He shut his eyes, tears forming, and said, "I guess I'll be in here."

It ended up being almost three and a half years that Michael spent in the detention center while the attorneys prepared for the trial. During all that time, I never had physical contact with him. I never even touched his hand. Eventually I found out that visiting was by television monitors because everyone there was awaiting trial, and they did not have the funds to staff a regular visiting room. The penal system only follows their rules; they never think of the impact of the loss of physical contact with your family. I could not imagine what all that time without any human contact could do to someone.

About six months after he got there, he came to visitation in a black-and-white-striped prison jumpsuit instead of the orange one. It was so ridiculous it was almost funny. It looked like a costume for a cartoon character. When I asked why he was wearing it, he said they now considered everyone in their group dangerous and wanted them to be highly visible. He had been moved into solitary confinement along with the other Aryan Warriors and now had outside privileges limited to just one hour a day in a caged, concrete exercise area. They would get to have a shower every three days. It would stay that way for the rest of his incarceration there. I wrote to the prison warden, but his secretary just wrote back that this was how Michael and the others were being kept due to their level of risk. I hated that striped outfit and what it represented for him.

Not long after the change in his uniform, his prison situation became worse when one of the Aryan Warriors attacked another with a homemade shiv at the telephone station. That particular inmate had been targeted because he was about to turn federal witness in their trial in order to get a better deal for himself. The gang members all maintain a code of behavior, and in that code, no one snitches, no matter what. That is probably the worst offense you can commit against other gang members. For them it is like turning your family in.

Because of the stabbing incident, the guards had them all strip to their underwear, told them to lie on the floor, and then hosed them down with water and left them to freeze for days. No clothes and no blankets, even though it was winter. They got their clothes back after two awful weeks, but were not let out at all, even for exercise, for several weeks more.

How could someone treat a human being like that...like an animal? I wrote to the warden again, but this time did not even get a response. By then Michael had made friends with some of the guards, and one of them told me Michael had not participated in the stabbing, but had been punished the same way because he was part of the gang. In prison, that's the way it works. In fact, in most prisons, if there is an altercation or fighting on the yard, they may lock down the entire prison while they sort out who is responsible and what happened, even though 98 percent of the inmates were not even involved. Because of this type of thinking and actions, inmates become more and more resentful, leading to more violence and more problems.

In the meantime, I started to hear news about the trial. I had no idea it was such a huge trial for the federal government until I saw articles in the newspaper and on television. The television stations took the story and ran with it day after day. It was sensational. I could not believe Michael was included in the violent and terrible things perpetrated by the Aryan Warrior gang. He had only been in the same prison at Ely for a few months, but he had been a member of the gang the whole time he was incarcerated at High Desert State Prison. The gang's tentacles were everywhere.

I attended the trial, but unlike other relatives and friends, I sat in the back and did not talk to reporters after any of the sessions. No one knew me or even paid attention to me. It was a blessing. For once, feeling invisible was a good thing.

I had been embarrassed at first, knowing some of my friends might see Michael's face on television or in the paper, but when I saw the mug shot I hardly recognized the angry, mean-looking young man depicted in the photo. Most likely the few of my friends who even knew Michael would not recognized him either. If they alienated themselves from me over this, then they really weren't friends.

By then I had remarried, and fortunately my husband, Ethan, was tolerant of Michael and his problems. They had met a few times when Michael was still on the outside. Those were treasured memories. At dinner, Michael had been his usual funny self, making quick-witted conversation. At times like those, I could almost believe he would be able to succeed. I always kept hoping that age would catch up with him and calm him down enough to let him live a semi-normal life. Even at the trial, I was thinking about whether there would be any hope for him in the future in spite of all this.

My husband did not attend the trial. He was working, but he supported me at home and listened to my renditions of what had happened, and how badly I felt, and how afraid I was for Michael. The trial itself was like a TV show. The federal courtroom was impressive, with polished wooden pew seats and flags in the front of the room behind the judge's podium. The defendants' attorneys and all the prosecuting attorneys outnumbered the defendants and the spectators. In addition, security was very tight; even if I had wanted to sit in the front row, I could not, as the guards would not let anyone near the defendants. There had been a rumor floating around about reprisal, so the government was afraid of violence from someone on the outside. There also had been possible threats against witnesses for the prosecution. An air of tight tension filled the room. Everyone was searched prior to entering the courthouse.

The defendants all had their hands and feet shackled. Guards accompanied them into the courtroom, wearing guns and Tasers. These were not old, fat court bailiff types, but muscular young men who watched every move in the courtroom. They were serious, and I knew they would not stand for any infractions of the rules.

Fortunately, no one ever showed up but the poor, miserable relatives and girlfriends. Once or twice girlfriends of Michael's showed up, but I just said hello and minded my own business. They had read about the trial in the newspaper or had seen the stories on television or on the Internet. Most of them had drug problems themselves, and I was not able to handle any more stress than I already had. Besides, I knew they would disappear after the commotion of the trial. They were there for him, but also for themselves just in case they might get seen on TV.

In the detention center, I had spoken with family members of the other men in Michael's trial, and we all shared the same sad story. None of us could quite figure out how or why our sons, husbands, or boyfriends had come to this. Some of the families did not even understand the gravity of the situation. They had no idea their loved one would soon spend a decade or more, maybe even life, in prison.

No one had the means to hire a private attorney without risking their home or life savings. Michael had been appointed a court attorney; I had never paid for an attorney for him, and even if I'd had the means

I would not have done so. He was a grown man and had made his own choices. However, I don't believe it would have mattered anyway. The government had plenty of proof of the years of illegal activities and violence perpetrated by the Aryan Warriors inside and outside Nevada prisons. It had been a long, thorough investigative process.

The charges all stemmed from the time Michael and the others were at Ely State Prison. Because he had been a member of the gang then and had continued supporting them on the outside, he had been included in all the charges. The district attorney indicted them with bribing corrections officers in order to facilitate their various criminal activities inside and outside prison, the murder of the inmate at Ely State Prison, assaults and stabbings of other prisoners, sale and distribution of drugs, and the use of labs gang members operated outside prison to produce methamphetamine. In addition, the FBI had proof that the gang had coerced some of the guards or that the guards had willingly participated in some of the illegal activities. The government was dealing with the guards in a separate trial.

The evidence amounted to hundreds of thousands of pages. The filing boxes of evidence were wheeled in on large dollies stacked as high as they could go. Originally there had been fourteen defendants. One of them became the state witness; he was the one who had been stabbed when the gang members found out he would be testifying against them. He had survived the attack and had been kept in separate, supervised confinement. The head shot caller of the gang was tried separately for the attempted murder. He was already serving a life sentence for the murder of a 7-Eleven store clerk. Six of the gang members struck plea bargain agreements just before the trial. That left six to stand trial. Among those was my son, considered a midlevel member of the gang.

On my monthly visit, I spoke to Michael about the trial and what might happen to him. He was scared of what the outcome would be. As he saw the others take deals, he was afraid the burden of the trial would land on him and the other defendants who were left. The newspapers and television stations laced their accounts with high drama, which seemed to make the whole thing appear worse than it already was.

In the end, all of them were convicted or pleaded guilty and took whatever deal they could. Michael was one of those who pleaded guilty during the trial, and he was sentenced to twelve or more years in the federal prison system for his crimes.

The next time I visited, I asked him why he had pleaded guilty. What he told me made sense. If the trial got to the point where the judge would be the final one to dictate the sentence, he thought that he would get a lot more time. That is what his attorney had told him, too. I thought about this. I knew that the district attorney and the prosecutors on the team had seemed determined to put them all away for the rest of their lives, and the media had splashed news about the trial all over the television, Internet, and newspapers for weeks. One of the articles said Michael was the Aryan Warrior "meth cook." That was the headline. He had not cooked any methamphetamine at all during that period, but had been guilty of selling it to an undercover cop. He probably made the right decision to plead guilty and take the sentence the district attorney offered.

CHAPTER 22

RICO CASE DOCUMENTS

After the trial, Michael asked me if I would keep his final RICO court documents if he sent them to me. He seemed to want them in case he needed to refer to them in the future. Maybe he was thinking that he might get an appeal. They arrived about two weeks later, stuffed in two medium-sized office file boxes. There must have been thousands of pages.

I decided to look through them before I stored them. As I read, I was astounded at the amount of surveillance the authorities had used to make their case. Obviously, I hadn't realized everything he had been doing, but I also never knew the extent to which the officials were watching him. It had begun long before his incarceration.

When he first got out of High Desert he had been living on the straight side of life, so they had not bothered with him then. It was only after he started his illegal activities again that they had begun their surveillance. High Desert State Prison and Ely State Prison officials had also copied all incoming mail for the Aryan Warriors, including Michael's. The letters were part of the case for the prosecution.

The letters to and from the gang members were written to make it appear that the letter was coming from the outside, instead of from a prison or jail. They had to be deciphered as code names were used for inmates and activities. A "brother" is always a member of the gang, and a "kite" is a note to someone. A job on the outside might really be a job in the prison. Someone going to college would actually be taking classes in the prison. If a letter said someone had lost their way, it meant they probably had tried to leave the gang. If someone said they were looking for a new job, it meant they were being transferred. Some of the codes were even more complicated; the first letter of every sentence would translate to a word, or the last letter of the sentence would reveal the word.

All jails and prison systems have networks of communication used by inmates to send information to one another. The methods are ingenious and as varied as the situation calls for. In solitary confinement, inmates might communicate just by talking from one cell to another. Then when someone gets out of solitary, that inmate passes information on to the general population. Sometimes they pass notes by throwing a weighted "line" of dental floss with the note attached down the cellblock. Later the information may be passed to a visitor who will call someone else, keeping the chain going until the information reaches the intended person.

Mail is another way to get information from one person to another. Because inmates are not permitted to write to one another, mail is usually sent to a friend or family member, and then that person sends the letter on. It is surprising how quickly a message can get around the country. All of this is against prison rules, but there really is no way to stop it.

Michael had asked me on many occasions to pass on letters. Mostly they were to female inmates at the women's prison in Las Vegas, but apparently some had been letters to other gang members. I had not realized at the time that codes were being used, and that I was participating by passing some of them on.

As I read through all the documents and letters, I saw a cast of drug users and dealers of every description, and they all seemed to be hooked on meth or heroin. Michael had been hanging around some pitiful people. Most of them had been incarcerated at one time or another. None had any means of making an honest living, and most of them either smoked meth or injected it. The rest were hooked on heroin. There were several so-called friends of Michael's, who turned over on him so they would get a better deal, and gave the FBI some of the information they needed to convict him. Then there were the girls hanging around, whom the police kept track of as well. They seemed to come and go as the wind blew.

The most interesting part was the recorded conversations between Michael and an undercover agent. The agent was good at what he did. Most conversations started with "Hey dude, what's happening." From there it was "Do you have any stuff? Where can I get some? Where can I meet you?" Michael was cautious, but after about fifteen calls and two failed meetings, one where Michael did not show and one where he did not have the goods, Michael had used one of the girls to make the fatal transfer in a parking lot.

I could not believe what I was reading. Michael is talking to the undercover cop, and he says, "How do I know you aren't with the police?"

The cop answers, "Because, dude, you know me. I've been around for ages."

Michael replies, "Yeah. Besides, I'm careful and I would know if you were undercover right away. I'm sure you are a stand-up guy."

I couldn't help but laugh. He was telling the undercover agent he would know if someone was a cop. It would be hilarious if it weren't so sad. Drugs make you think you are invincible. No wonder almost all addicts are caught eventually.

At one of the darkest points in his life, Michael's drug habit had become so bad that it had been costing him several hundred dollars a day, if not more. He would stay up for days at a time and then crash for days. He would take apart radios, motorcycles, and other electronics and never put them back together. At times, he had lost weight and his skin looked bad. Even his teeth, which had been beautiful, were damaged. If he had continued using any longer, he would have looked like the posters of meth addicts, with the sores on their skin and all their teeth broken or missing.

Meth keeps you from caring about anything, including your health. How can you remember to brush your teeth if you can't think straight? If it can erode away the enamel on your teeth, imagine what it does to your brain. Chronic use changes the brain structure and may cause anxiety, violent behavior, confusion, psychosis, and impaired cognitive ability. Users often become paranoid and incredibly hyperactive. It is as if they are running at full speed until they crash and burn.

Being caught probably saved Michael's life...for whatever life he would have in prison.

CHAPTER 23

FCI TUCSON, ARIZONA AND FCI EDGEFIELD, SOUTH CAROLINA

After his sentencing, Michael had asked to be transferred somewhere near Las Vegas, but they sent him to the Tucson Federal Correctional Facility in Arizona. About two months after he arrived there, my husband and I made the hot seven-hour drive to Tucson. We rented a motel and prepared for the visit the next day.

The Tucson prison is modern, but still looks threatening. When we arrived there, the guards would not let me in because my sandals did not have backs on them, even though we told them how far we had come. There was no compassion. I was upset that they would use what I thought was a frivolous rule and make me go out and purchase shoes, after I had traveled so far. It was not as if I was breaking an important rule or exposing any part of my body. I had always tried to follow the rules. There are many other regulations for which they can deny entry: you cannot wear a short skirt, shorts, backless or sleeveless blouse, underwire bra, dresses above the knees or with a slit, or sagging pants. Certainly some of them make sense, but backs on your sandals? Still, I knew not to cause trouble; they have the power to not let you in, and don't even have to tell you the reason.

After driving a couple of miles to Walmart for a different pair of shoes, we returned and went through a series of locked doors to the visiting room. There Michael and I were finally able to meet face to face after over three years. It was a very emotional moment for both of us.

During that time, I had only seen Michael through a television monitor or in court. We had not even held hands. Now I finally had the opportunity to give him an actual hug and a kiss. It's funny how the ability to have personal touch makes a difference. Unfortunately, the inmate who loses contact visits also loses them for his family.

Michael was in high spirits. He said this was a vacation hotel in Hawaii compared to the North Las Vegas Detention Center.

"It is like being let into Disneyland with a ticket to all the rides. Really, it feels incredible just to see the sky. I have not seen the sky without a screen over it for years."

His appearance had not changed, so I was a little disappointed, but assumed it was probably what he had to do to keep his status in the gang. Considering what he had been through the past few years, he looked good. When he was in court, he had looked stressed, and while he had been in the North Las Vegas Detention Center, he had just looked beaten. Now he seemed happy. He immediately went into his joke routine and talked about everything that had happened since the trial. He asked my husband how he was, and kept the conversation going for hours with his unique ability to keep things upbeat.

We had a good visit and ate the usual vending machine junk food. Michael's favorites were always Dr. Pepper and Cheetos—after he had eaten about three cheeseburgers. They were like heaven to him. The prison food is so bland that food from the vending machines tastes like a gourmet dinner. It was the same at High Desert State Prison and probably in all prisons. The penal system only requires facilities to supply certain amounts of nutrition, and taste doesn't matter.

Despite Michael's good humor, the visit was an emotional one for me, because Michael was now in a federal facility. Just the thought of it sounded more intimidating than his being in state prison, even though the facility itself was not more threatening than High Desert State Prison had been. It was just the idea that he was a federal prisoner now. Maybe it sounded final in some way, as if he had graduated to a place that was worse than the one he had been in.

We stayed another day, because it didn't make sense to go all that way and not take advantage of the two-day visiting period. The second day went a little easier. The guards were a bit friendlier, and as they guided us into the visiting area, they were smiling and chatting with the other visitors. One of them even made a joke about our previous day's trip to Walmart.

In the end, we didn't mind Tucson so much, after all the time he had spent in the North Las Vegas Detention Center. At least it wasn't a no-contact visiting facility, and because it was small, the visiting room seemed friendlier. Family members do not get a say in where their loved one is incarcerated, so we felt fortunate to be able to visit Michael there, even though it was a long trip. At least we could travel by car to get there.

Michael ended up staying in Tucson for just eighteen months. I don't know why he was transferred, but in the federal prisons there is a system of points and gang relationships the prison administration looks at. They move inmates around to break up gangs and keep them from becoming too strong in any one facility. Michael asked to be sent near Las Vegas again, and this time they sent him to Edgefield, South Carolina—just about as far away from Las Vegas as you can get. The prison system has no regard for the families of prisoners. They make no exceptions for anyone, and just follow their placement rules.

His transfer took almost three months to complete. During those three months, they moved him from facility to facility. It is not cost effective to move only a few inmates at a time, so they move them to central transfer points until they have enough prisoners in one place going to the next.

If the next place is nearby, they will be moved by bus. They cuff the high-risk offenders with their hands in a box and feet shackled to the floor. The others are just cuffed to the seat. If they move prisoners by plane, they cuff them to benches and put the high-risk offenders into cages within the plane. I was shocked and angry to hear that they had transported Michael as a high-risk offender in a cage. He had never tried to escape, attacked a guard, or been convicted of a violent crime against others. His past record and affiliation with the Aryan Warriors was what had earned him this special treatment. If the plane had crashed or burned, he would not have had a chance to escape. He would have been dead.

Because of the distance, we were only able to visit him in South Carolina once. Fortunately, they allowed the inmates to use email. The federal system has the technology to allow it, so we communicated almost daily that way. One of the first things Michael wrote about was how hot and humid it was there. He said that when he worked out, he would be drenched in sweat. He was not used to the humidity. He did complain that there were not as many educational opportunities there, but he could work in the Unicor program, a private enterprise that uses inmates to work for them. He was looking forward to that, because he could earn money.

Michael seemed happy about where he was, aside from the humidity found in the South. He was full of stories about the opportunity to work for Unicor. It is a win-win situation; the company gets cheap labor, and the inmates have the chance to learn skills and keep a job while in prison. They make uniforms, bulletproof vests, carry bags for soldiers, and a lot of other military apparel. He made sixty-five cents an hour at his job and was due for a promotion. He also had money to spend in the commissary. Money for commissary is very important when you are incarcerated. It is your only way to get something different to eat, vitamins, clothes, and electronics. Most inmates don't have anyone who can afford to, or will send them money for commissary, so they have to earn it.

There are a limited number of jobs available inside prisons, and Unicor paid more than the others. You can work in the kitchen, landscaping, library, or laundry, or as a trustee or porter. I think all inmates should have a job and contribute to the operation of the facility that is holding them. And if an inmate does take one of the jobs available, they might be able to transfer those skills to the outside. A kitchen worker may be able to get a job in a restaurant. The landscaper could start their own landscaping business when they get out. At least they have developed some skills and have learned to work with others, which is probably something few inmates have ever done before.

During his incarceration at FCI Tucson, he had taken several business classes. I knew that if he combined his education with his work experience in FCI Edgefield, he would at least have some work skills and business knowledge he could take with him when he was released.

CHAPTER 24

LEGACY OF ABANDONMENT

It was during Michael's stay in South Carolina that the letter arrived—a letter from a granddaughter I had never met. I had been expecting it for some time, but never really wanted to think about it. Michael had told me about her a few of years previously. She was the child of a schoolmate from junior high school, a woman who had been in and out of his life for many years. Their daughter had to be about twenty years old now.

It was a letter that I was supposed to pass on to Michael. I knew I shouldn't open it, but I did.

What I read was devastating. The writing was childlike, with back-slanted printing and lots of smiley faces and LOLs. Nevertheless, the girl spoke of her mother and her own daughter, a great-grandchild I never knew I had.

Her own mother had serious health problems. She had been in and out of the hospital due to health problems from doing crystal meth. Her drug use had ruined her health and life. She faced death unless she changed her ways. Even now, she was still using drugs, never went to visit her own daughter, or even gave her a phone number to reach her.

My granddaughter wrote about these things in a matter-of-fact manner, as if they were everyday happenings. How she herself was a heroin addict, how she had been in the hole for two months now, how everyone was against her. How she misses her child—my great-granddaughter—who was in the care of relatives. She told Michael how she doesn't care that her mother does not visit her or communicate with her. She wrote,

"Whatever..."—the all-encompassing phrase people use when they are pretending nothing is important to them.

This girl was caught in a circle of drug use and abuse. No father around and no mother who could be counted on. She herself was fulfilling the role almost destined to her. Now her child did not have a father or mother. Would that child follow the same path?

Then she wrote, "Happy birthday, Dad. I know you turned 40." It's then I began to cry. Forty wasted years, and now it was continuing with yet another child. This one did not even get the chance for one stable parent. By the time she signed off with little Xs and Os, I could barely see through my tears. All I could see was the never-ending circle of rejection, drug abuse and lack of respect for anything or anyone.

The very thing that hurt him so much as a child, his father leaving him and losing contact, was exactly what he was doing to his children. Yes, he professed to love them, and I knew he did, but what help had he ever given to them or their mothers? What support had he ever shown them?

The mother of his daughter, Sarah, has a full-time job twenty-four hours a day taking care of her. Girls with Rett syndrome have health problems for life. If anything, it gets harder as the years go by. Sarah was a young adult now, and although these girls stay small in stature and frame, it was no longer easy to lift her. She also had frequent seizures, and her bouts of pneumonia were worse every year, too. It was an ongoing battle to keep her healthy.

The State of California provides support and funds for her daily care and her medical care. That is fortunate, but how often had Michael stayed up making sure the feeding tube was okay? How many times had he gone to the doctor's with her? When did he go to school meetings, or to meetings with state officials? How many letters had he written on her behalf to make sure she continued to receive state aid? How much had he contributed to the daily grind that can take one's soul away?

How many times had Michael been there for his son, Danny, or his son's mother? How much had he contributed to his son's education and well-being? Had he ever attended a school or sports event? Where was he when his son's friends asked where his father was? Where was he when Danny learned how to drive and graduated from high school and then from university? There had been a few phone calls and emails between them, but that did not add up to any kind of real relationship. It was heartbreaking that Michael was doing to his son exactly what his father had done to him.

Little children forget, and the older ones are often resentful of the bleak hole caused by the absence of their parent. Who could blame them? They have a parent who chose to live a life of crime, resulting in imprisonment, instead of taking care of their families. That is the truth, no matter which way you slice it. They have failed their families in every way. You can sit in any waiting room and see the inmates' children, some with their heads hanging down and some acting out. The kids feel deserted and often have a lack of self-esteem because of it, leading them, in some cases, to carry on the same kind of life. It is the sorriest story of all. Eventually they stop coming to visit.

CHAPTER 25

USP BEAUMONT

After almost eighteen months in South Carolina, Michael called to say they were transferring him to a high-risk facility in Beaumont, Texas. I was glad that it was closer and easier to get to. He was not happy; he said it was a high-risk facility and a terrible place.

"How can you know that when you haven't even arrived there yet?"

"Mom, it won't be good for me. We hear things about every place. There are gangs there that are the worst in the system. They even have the Mexican Mafia Black Hand gang there."

I didn't know what that was, but it sounded dangerous. Still, there was nothing I could do. "What happened that you are being transferred?"

"Here's what happened. These Mexican dudes beat up on one of the white guys. Now the warden hears there is going to be retaliation, so he throws all the Aryans into the hole, and then makes arrangements to have all twelve of us transferred. I told my caseworker I wasn't involved, and he knew that, but against the warden there was nothing he could do. Mom, I swear I did not do anything. You can call my caseworker, and he will tell you straight up that I am telling the truth."

I was doubtful, so I took the number and called the next day. The caseworker told me that Michael had not participated in the threat or the talk, but because he was part of the gang, he was sent to the hole too. When I asked the caseworker why he was being sent to a high-risk prison, he told me Michael had a detainer from the State of Nevada that had caught up with him, for a case he still had in the state. In that case, they had classified him as a habitual criminal. This was a case tied up with the same charges from the federal Aryan Warrior case. Apparently the State of Nevada had entered charges against him at the state level, too.

I was overwhelmed. I was afraid the violence he would encounter in Texas might lead to him doing something himself and getting more charges on his record. Worse, he might end up remaining in prison the rest of his life. He had been doing so well, taking college classes in Tucson and working for Unicor in South Carolina. He'd had just one write-up for behavior problems in all the years since his conviction. How did that translate into a reason for them to send him to a high-security facility instead of a medium-security prison?

The caseworker said, "It doesn't make sense, but they just see things the way they do, and I can't do anything about what the department that makes the determination says. They just look at their level of assigned points based on their record. If you ask me, this time he is getting a raw deal, but you didn't hear that from me."

The next day I emailed the department responsible for the placement determinations, and they responded with a formal email saying that according to their rules, because of the number of points he had and because of his state case, he had to go to a high-level facility.

USP Beaumont is about a hundred miles east of Houston, thirty-five miles north of the Gulf of Mexico, and about four miles south of the city of Beaumont. There is not a lot to say for the city of Beaumont. There are five prison complexes in the area, and so many refineries that you can smell the oil in the air. Smokestacks spew out thick white clouds of smoke, and if you have any respiratory problems, they are exacerbated just by being outside.

USP Beaumont is in a complex consisting of low, medium, and high-security facilities. There are over 5,600 inmates within the complex, but the high-security USP site, where they were sending Michael, houses between 1,400 and 1,500 inmates. Razor wire and eight high gun towers surround it.

Over the years, Beaumont has housed some famous inmates, including one of the Somali pirates convicted of hijacking the American yacht, SY Quest, and killing four hostages, a hedge fund manager who stole over $100 million from more than eight hundred investors, and a Louisiana senator convicted of money laundering and stealing from an insurance company. It also housed some of the infamous Mexican Mafia members, reportedly the most vicious of all prison gangs.

It is an intimidating facility, both outside and in. The reputation for violence is well deserved, due to the number of violent gangs who make it their home. One year, more than half the inmates were transferred to other facilities because of the fights, stabbings, gang wars, and violence seen there on an everyday basis. I wondered whether in that environment, Michael might become violent himself and rely more and more on his gang affiliations to protect him. The chances of his getting killed were greater, too.

I got a collect call as soon as he arrived. "Mom, I can't stay here. This place is the worst place ever. There are people here who are animals, and they do not care what happens to them or anyone else. I have never seen such violence as there is here."

"What kind of violence?"

His voice shook. "Just every kind. Stabbings, rapes, fights, everything. These guys are dangerous. Most of them have life, so they don't care what happens. They seem to want to bring others down to their level. If I stay here I will either get killed or be in trouble forever."

"Then you just have to find a way to stay away from them. Get a job and do the best you can. Hold your temper, keep your head down, and don't let them get the best of you."

The next call, just a few days later, was the same thing. But after a while he seemed to settle down and not be as scared as he was. I later discovered why. The informal process for a new inmate is for them to prove themselves when they arrive. They have to present their "papers" so the inmates who are already there know they are not a snitch or a sexual offender. Michael had asked me to send copies of his federal court case to someone in Texas, who I assume sent it on or provided validation that he was who he said he was, and did what he said he did. At the time, I did not know about this, and it made me feel a little like I had been duped into participating. After I thought about it for a few days, I realized that if I had not done it, he might have been in big trouble. I found it somewhat ironic, a big guy like him afraid, but then I wasn't there. The Aryans in Beaumont would have his back, but at what cost?

Meant to house some of the worst offenders in the United States, USP Beaumont was a hellhole. Several inmates were murdered within those walls over the years. One former inmate wrote on his blog that he was witness to stabbings and beatings on a daily basis, and that they were on lockdown so frequently that visiting was a crapshoot. He was there about eight years before Michael arrived, and he said it was the worst prison he was in during his ten-year sentence. Another said he'd watched ambulances leave there on a weekly basis.

According to Leah Caldwell, writing in *Prison Legal News*, USP Beaumont got the nickname of "Thunder Dome" (based on the movie depicting apocalyptic gladiators fighting to the death in a cage) because rival prisoners had been put into a fifteen-by-twenty-foot recreation cage and allowed to fight each other.[3] In 2001, one of the inmates fighting in the cage died when the other inmate stomped on his head. This was the fifth murder since 1997 in that facility.

A detailed 2009 article from the beaumontenterprise.com paper related the stabbing and death of an informant a day after he transferred to Beaumont.[4] Another inmate had stabbed him 106 times in the chest. The perpetrator was facing a possible death sentence.

In addition, Beaumont had a reputation for the highest rate of positive drug tests in the entire Federal Bureau of Prisons. To get drugs into a high-security prison like Beaumont usually takes the cooperation of the guards. This reminded me that Michael was partially in the place

---

3 Leah Caldwell, "USP Beaumont, Texas: Murder and Mayhem in the Thunder Dome," *Prison Legal News* 16, no. 9 (2005): 10–11, https://www.prisonlegalnews.org/news/2005/sep/15/usp-beaumont-texas-murder-and-mayhem-in-the-thunder-dome/.

4 Collin Guy, "Man Gets Death Penalty for Murder of Fellow Inmate at Beaumont Prison," *beaumontenterprise.com*, May 18, 2009, http://www.beaumontenterprise.com/news/article/Man-gets-death-penalty-for-murder-of-fellow-745093.php.

he was because of how the Aryan Warriors had bribed guards at High Desert and Ely State Prisons.

Violence and drugs were not the only problems at Beaumont. Past inmates had complained about the food, treatment of inmates, medical care, and other issues. A *Houston Press* news article chronicled one inmate's attempt to sue the Federal Bureau of Prisons after Hurricane Rita.[5] Inmate Deetz said the low-level inmates were evacuated, but the maximum-security inmates were left locked in their cells for days, with only plastic bags for toilets, nothing to eat but bologna sandwiches, and barely any water to drink. The inmates felt helpless and were terrified of dying in their cells as the 175 mph hurricane approached Beaumont. In the aftermath, they spent weeks with only the sandwiches to eat, no toilet facilities, and no air conditioning. When relatives called the Federal Bureau of Prisons, they were told the inmates were fine and that there was nothing to worry about. It took Deetz almost two years to file his complaint.

Michael arrived there in 2011, so several years of better conditions had been in place, and by 2008, Beaumont had relocated most of the hardcore inmates to other facilities. However, according to the president of the local union for federal prison workers at that time, the violence was partly caused by lack of staff and few behavioral incentives for the inmates.[6] I was not sure things had changed that much, especially given Michael's description of what continued to happen there.

"Why don't you get a job with Unicor?" I asked, thinking that if he was working there he might keep out of trouble.

He said he couldn't because the Aryans had told him, in no uncertain terms, that he had to be on the yard in case they needed him. If trouble started, he had to participate with the rest of the gang. They were a small group compared to some of the other gangs, so they needed all

---

5 Chris Vogel, "A Prison Cover-Up during Hurricane Rita," *Houston Press News*, March 5, 2008, http://www.houstonpress.com/2008–03–06/news/a-prison-coverup-during-hurricane-rita/.
6 Ryan Meyers, "FCC Beaumont: Hardcore Cons Move Out," *Enterprise (TX)*, April 6, 2006, http://www.november.org/cstayinfo/breaking08/HardcoreBeaumont.html.

the members they could get to be available. The Unicor job would have taken him off the yard during the day.

"What do you mean? Are they telling you what to do?"

"They are, and it is really bad because now I can't earn any money. They did say I could get a job with landscaping, and that way I will be available and still have a job. The only problem is that the landscaping job only earns about eight dollars a week, and with Unicor I was earning sixty-five cents an hour. Big difference."

I did not hear from him for over two weeks after that, and became concerned. I thought he might have gotten himself put in the SHU. Finally he called and said the entire facility had been locked down for two weeks. There had been some fights and a stabbing on the yard, and tension was still so high that they only let the inmates out for an hour or so each day until things cooled down.

He said it was a common occurrence at this facility. The inmates were constantly shouting and posturing, and there was even shooting from the towers. They didn't always use rubber bullets, either.

Michael's stay at Beaumont USP looked like it would be his most challenging yet. I could only pray he would keep himself together and make it through in one piece. At least he had email, and we could communicate frequently.

CHAPTER 26

LETTER FROM THE PAST

While Michael was in Beaumont, Jennifer told me she had written a letter to him. Would it be okay if she sent it? This was a surprise to me, as she had not really spoken to him or seen him in fifteen or twenty years or more, but I had kept in constant contact with her and my grandson.

I gave her the address, and then I asked her if I could read the letter too. She emailed it to me. I was blown away. It was a poignant letter from someone who never truly gave up on Michael. It was true she had not had anything to do with him for years, as most of his friends hadn't, but it was a positive gesture for her to want to communicate with him now.

Inmates who are cut off from all communication with the outside have less chance of ever being able to function in normal society. I had encouraged his son and a few others to keep in touch with Michael, but over the years, I really was the only one who bothered. Once in a while he would get a few letters from a girl or two he had known. Most of them were incarcerated too, and when they got out he never heard from them again. That's why pen pals for inmates are important. They provide a lifeline to the outside and help inmates remember that there is a life outside those walls. It gives them hope enough to realize they might be able to live and function in society again someday.

Jennifer emailed the letter to me.

Hey Michael, knucklehead ;}

Funny thing. When I get bored at work, I end up doing stupid things and today was one of those days. For whatever reason, I searched your name. I wasn't really thinking about you particularly, just had this random notion. Stupid huh!

Well, there popped up a couple of pictures of you. The first one was fairly "normal" whatever the hell your normal is. (?) :]

The second however, I couldn't place. I couldn't for some reason believe in my heart that is you. I mean, I know it is but it hit me in somewhat of a sad way. I stopped, closed the browser, leaned back in my chair and started to think (deeply) how in the hell you went from a guy that used to lay behind me and sing to me; or be at the end of my delivery bed acting like you were going to catch a football when I was in labor with Danny :D

You had so much going for you!

You are so smart. Maybe too smart sometimes (not so smart on some things-eyes rolling ;) You have always had this great sense of humor and quick wit. Thoughtful beyond most men's capability . . . sweet and a good listener. Fun and exciting always wanting to show me a good time. (Except the banshees in the desert-that wasn't very nice) I look at that scowl in the picture of you. I remember it. The sadness behind it, but it's changed. Not the sadness, but that now-there's actually hate in your face and it affects me in a way of sadness so deep. I don't know you anymore. Haven't in many years, but in this strange "family, brotherly, awkward love" feeling; I love you and I'm so sad for your life. I know that I, nor anyone else, could have saved you. God knows we have all tried. But, what I wonder is: in your down time, what do you think about? What were your goals? Did you have any? Do you have any now? Have you thought about any kind of "normal" future you might have? Or, is it still "going down in a blaze of glory"?

What is it? What does it all mean? Stand for? What is your gain? What does YOUR LIFE mean? How do you look at yourself in the mirror every day and not question why? And then try REALLY hard to seek the answers. YOU ARE LOVED!!!! PEOPLE LIKE YOU!!! GUESS WHAT? We all love and like you-GUESS WHY? Because you have always been precious and admired and adored by us! Not because of what you had or didn't have, but because we genuinely liked you!

I just sit here at my desk and wonder for your future-brother (awkward but that's how I feel for you now. Like a pesky little brother-just not so little :} . . . What do you see?

Find goals that give your life meaning. Give yourself back what you have robbed yourself of.

Find love. Real love. Not based on perversion and sex, but honor and decency. Loyalty and respect. I hope that for you. I hope you give yourself your freedom back and enjoy the rest of your life happily. Find normalcy. Find your own peace. Nothing matters at this point-other than peace and quiet in yourself. In your heart. Put a smile back on that mug!!! Lol!

Your sister and forever friend,

Jennifer

—ɯ—

I was glad she wrote, if even for the one time.

CHAPTER 27

VISITING USP BEAUMONT

It was some time before I was able to manage a visit to Beaumont. The prison was on lockdown frequently, and visiting was not allowed during that time. Usually some misguided inmate had stabbed another, probably over something stupid like a cigarette. It was prison, and there was no way out, so what did they think they would accomplish? Settle a score? What could be so important? Then there were always those who wanted to make sure a child molester or a snitch never saw the light of day again. I did not care. I just wanted to be able to visit.

At least my tickets were refundable this time. I had tried earlier in the year to visit, but the prison had been on lockdown, and I was not able to go. Stupidly, I had bought non-refundable plane tickets. It's no wonder families don't visit when their relatives are in a federal prison far away from home. It costs a lot of money, and for some families the plane fare and even gasoline for a road trip are prohibitive.

Ethan made the trip with me. We flew to Houston, and then rented a car and drove the hundred or more miles to Beaumont. It was very humid, and the muted skies looked like rain. I was happy to have my husband along this time; for once, I did not want to journey alone. It brought back memories of all the times I had driven to High Desert State Prison alone.

As we approached the mammoth prison on Knauth Road, we became quiet. It was just as I had imagined it from Michael's description of the gun towers and massive fencing. It was the most depressing facility Michael had been in yet. Even the sky above was depressing, dressed in colors of blue and gray. I could understand why he hated it there so much.

When we arrived at the prison, even though I was looking forward to the visit, my anxiety level was so high that I had to stop and close my eyes for a moment. The guard at the desk was huge, over six feet tall, and seemed to glare at me through his glasses. I realized I was holding my breath while he checked my husband's identification and then mine. Finally he let us in. We followed the rest of the visitors through the fences and walkways to the visiting room.

When Michael walked in, I saw he had not shaved off his beard or grown his hair out. His goatee was now prematurely gray, and he looked menacing with his bald head now completely covered in tattoos. Nevertheless, he was smiling from ear to ear.

I moved to give him a hug, and one of the guards yelled for me to get back. What had happened? I know I looked surprised as I turned to go back to my place. I had not known all visitors had to wait for a signal from a guard to move into the visiting area. I felt humiliated, so I placed myself behind my husband, just relieved that they had not made us leave. It had been a very long time since I'd had the chance to visit.

"I'm so glad to see you, Michael. You look good in spite of your head. I see whoever tattooed your head followed your hairline. The design makes you look like you have hair from a distance."

He embraced me with a long, tight hug and then shook hands with Ethan, laughing at my comment. "I'm glad to see you too, mamasita."

He would call me "mamasita" when he was in a playful mood. I could tell by his wide smile and the way he talked that he was happy for the visit. We talked about all the things that had being going on with us and with him. He had graduated from his virtual welding class and was happy to have another class he could put on his record before his state parole hearing the next spring. He had also registered for a computer class that started the next month.

After we had talked for a while, he told us about how he was helping call the shots for the Aryan Brotherhood there at Beaumont. I was not too happy to hear that, and my face reflected it.

Of course he noticed my expression. "Mom, I have to do what I have to do. You know that. At least when I'm involved, there isn't as much violence. I even have a new rule that members of the gang have to get their GED. When all those white boys began to register for classes, the chief honcho corrections officer asked me what the hell was going on. They thought we might be going to start some kind of action. I just told them if you belong to this gang, you have to have some sense. You can't be a dumb-ass white boy."

"At least that's something. Any education is better than none," I said. "You're doing a good thing by initiating that rule."

It still made me worry that he might be letting himself in for trouble. If everything is going okay, there aren't any problems for the shot caller, but if things go wrong, they might be targeted by another gang member or even one of their own.

"Yeah, sometimes some of the young ones don't think things out. Yesterday one of them came to me for permission to trounce a guy just because the guy didn't hang up the phone he was waiting for on time. What? Dude, you want to get in someone's face just because you thought you should be on the phone sooner? I told him no way. What an idiot. He could start a war over something as stupid as that."

While we were sitting there, I saw him watching everything that was going on. His eyes darted to each movement. He tensed up when any of the other inmates got up for a bathroom break. I wondered if this was a reflection of his new status and duties, or if it was the same old nerves he'd always had.

It was a good thing he had not seen the two inmates taking photos with their girlfriends in the area to the back of him. They stood close behind the women and pretended they were just taking photos, when they were really pressing up against them. I was disgusted that the guards just ignored it. There were children in the room, too. Michael probably would have gotten up in their faces, and then the visit would have been over for everyone. But what did I know; maybe those actions were not enough to warrant the guards initiating something. On the other hand, maybe the guards were just too lazy to interfere. Even though this was a high-level federal prison, I was surprised that the visiting area seemed more lenient than at High Desert State Prison.

Michael had been looking in our direction, and then abruptly he looked left into the room. Several guards entered and headed toward the back left side of the room.

"What's going on?" I asked as I turned to see where they were going.

"It's the drug enforcement squad. That idiot back there just got passed some dope, so now they'll take him back to the entry area, strip him, and bend him over. If they don't find anything, they will let him sit naked in that room until he shits."

My husband looked at Michael with a smile. "It isn't every day we get to see a takedown for drugs in the visiting area."

Michael laughed. "I guess not. Anyway, he deserves whatever he gets. And they will probably put his girlfriend in jail, too."

While we talked I noticed how he tapped his foot and chewed his nails as he always had, even when he was little. He had not broken those habits yet. I was distracted myself, thinking about how to talk to him about what he might do when he got out.

"I need to talk to you about something important," I said.

"What, you're moving to Miami to live with the rest of the old folks?"

"Well, that might happen, but it's more serious than that."

"Okay, it can't be that bad, so get it over with. You aren't sick, are you? You know the one thing I want is for you to still be hanging out when I get out of this hellhole." He leaned forward in his plastic chair.

"No, I'm not sick, but it is important. I'm concerned about what your plans are for when you get out. You haven't seemed to make any definite decisions about what you would like to do." I leaned back and Ethan took my hand.

"You know I've taken all the classes I can and have worked when I can. Even now, I have that stupid-ass job in landscaping. You have to cut me a break."

"I can cut you a break. I just don't see any of your counselors doing anything about helping you make your plans. I have not heard one word about reentry or a place for you to stay. Where is all the rehabilitation stuff they talk about on their websites?"

As he leaned back from me, Michael said, "I'll just have to keep after them. I don't know what else to do."

Ethan put his hand on my shoulder and looked at me as if to tell me to back off; Michael had a lot of anxiety about the subject already.

I didn't want to ruin the visit, so I left it at that. The prison system is rife with inefficiencies and bureaucratic red tape. Whenever I have contacted them with questions or problems, I have always gotten back standard answers saying that the rules were the guidelines they followed. However, they have not been responsive to Michael's asking about anything, not even transfers, rehabilitation, or a halfway house. They have just put him off, saying they could not tell him anything yet. I was anxious for Michael to get his plans for release in order ahead of time. I didn't think he would be getting any help from the prison system.

After you have been talking for five hours, no matter how long it has been since you have seen each other, you run out of things to say. Your only choice is to just sit there and look at each other, and since that is uncomfortable, we got ready to leave. The guards in the visiting room had been unsociable, but Michael still chatted them up as we were leaving. He had not lost his wit or his charm.

"I'll email you when we get home," I said. "It's a long ways, and we won't be home until late tonight. I love you. I had a great visit."

Michael just hugged me and then turned to return to the cellblock. "For sure, for sure. I'll email you too. I love you, Mom."

I watched him turn in his pass and walk toward the post-visit search room. He walked slowly, and I saw him turn slightly as if to see if we were still there. I waved, and then we turned to leave. Tears formed and fell quietly as we walked away. There wasn't anything I could do. He had to live his life. He was a grown man, more than forty years old, and only he could make the decisions that would be right for him.

CHAPTER 28

TIME MARCHES ON

As time goes by, life takes its toll. There is no stopping it. I couldn't get it out of my head when Michael told me his friend's mother had died. His friend had not seen his mother in several years and will never see her again. It's depressing how many family members die while their relatives are in prison, and it seems most of the time it is the mothers. How must it feel to lose the chance to say goodbye to or attend the funeral of your own mother? Yes, an inmate may be paying a debt to society, but the family also pays a debt by spending years without their loved one. Sometimes these are the last years they have left.

Thinking about the death of Michael's friend's mother reminds me that I too could be a casualty before Michael gets out of prison. I cannot think of anything more devastating than that for him. I have stopped taking chances. I look around in the parking lot for threats. I don't go near the edges of tall buildings, and I am cautious crossing the streets. I see the doctor if I have a lingering cough, and I get my annual checkup on time. I see the lines on my face increasing and the veins in my legs getting worse. I know I do not have the same endurance, or even the same drive for endurance. Sure, I can walk a few miles, and I exercise and try to eat healthy, but those things can only stay the tide of age for so long. I only hope that what I am doing will keep me here for when Michael gets out.

In 2011, my father-in-law had moved to Las Vegas after he became ill with heart disease, diabetes, and end-stage renal failure. His skin was like tissue paper. Every bump produced a wound. His thin, rope-veined arms and hands shook, but they spoke volumes about a life spent in hard work.

It is heartbreaking to see someone you love deteriorate right before your eyes. He became so weak and debilitated that he needed help with every aspect of daily life, even getting his laundry done, making his bed, and cleaning his house. He was no longer able to drive, and often stumbled and could not express easily what he wanted to say. At least I did not have to take the car keys away from him. Can you imagine not being able to just get in your car and go where and when you want to? It was as if he were in prison too.

Now he is on dialysis three times a week, and every day is a struggle for him. It has been a challenge to balance my life with his needs. There is a daily crisis of varying degrees. Sometimes he has fallen, or I need to take him to doctor's visits, or I must fill in when his dressings need changing. Sometimes it is just shopping and cooking. I know he cannot live alone anymore, and now the decision of when and how to move him in with us looms ahead.

As he fails, I see what the future could bring for me. It is terrifying. What if I become an invalid and am unable to take care of myself? Where will I be in ten or twenty years? I do not see as well as I once did; nor do I have the same energy as ten years ago. I do not feel as strong or as quick as before, and I have minor aches and pains on a weekly basis. I forget names and have a hard time remembering where I left my pencil or cup of coffee. I have to make a list to go to the store, or I forget what I really needed.

What role will Michael play in this aging process? Will he even be there to help? Will he be willing to help? I do not know the answers to that yet, and I can only hope he will. Maybe my fate will be a nursing home. How will Michael deal with it? Come to see me or not come to see me? I do not know, but there is nothing I can do to change the future.

I am not alone out here. There are thousands of other family members who are sick or dying, and they do not have any help or support from their loved ones in prison. No one ever talks about it. There are not a lot of solutions for family members who need help. They can only sit on the outside and wait, and sometimes that wait ends before their loved ones ever get out.

Michael has no other support system on the outside. Everyone has deserted him or no longer cares where or how he is. Even my family does not often ask about him. His own son hardly ever returns his emails. He succeeded in his life and is busy with work and friends. Michael has been away so long that they have all gone on with their lives. His fly-by-night friends are long gone and would not care even if they knew where he was. Some of them are even dead. One of them, a stripper from the days he worked at the strip clubs, committed suicide. His only support, besides me, is on the inside from the members of the gang he is in and supports. It is just how it is. Life goes on, and if you are not a part of it, you are left behind and forgotten.

Sometimes I think that if I did meet my demise before he gets out, it might actually be a good thing. He would no longer have support or someone to turn to. He would have to shift for himself without any help. On the other hand, if I am still here I can provide some support, maybe just enough that he could make it without resorting to old habits. He has told me in almost every email for the past few years that he is through with the life that brought him to prison. He has been drug-free for many years now. If conduct disorder is truly his condition, then age sometimes allows the person to change enough to function on the outside without resorting to criminal activities. On the other hand, some people with conduct disorder never get better. Their fate is to spend the rest of their days in prison.

CHAPTER 29

NATURE VERSUS NURTURE

I sometimes wonder how many of the two million or more people in American prisons share the same characteristics. Are their brains neurologically different than those of the general population? Time and time again, I have heard my son say he wished he had not lost his temper or reverted back to drugs, yet he did. Why was he not able to abstain from criminal acts? On the television program *Lockup*, you see prisoner after prisoner who has made the wrong choices repeatedly, even when they say they know better. You hear them talk about how to behave and then the next minute you see their anger erupt and they end up being sent to the SHU.

Over the years, I have communicated with some of Michael's friends who are also serving time. One of them is even serving a life sentence. Like Michael, they share similar stories. Most of them have been in trouble since they were young. Some of them come from families that have many different problems, and some even have family members who have been incarcerated. Usually they had difficulties in school and with authority figures. Sometimes their family has given up on them, and I am one of the few people they still communicate with. Occasionally they send me their artwork, which often is simply spectacular. The amount of time it must take for them to create such detailed work is incomprehensible. I have also received letters and poems that are so full of pain that they tear at my soul. They put all of their fears, pain, sorrow, and feelings of desolation into their artistic endeavors. With the talent they have, I can only wonder why and how they were not able to use their abilities to do something to sustain themselves on the outside.

I asked one of the inmates I have written to over the years if he would be willing to tell me how he got to where he is now. His story was a lot like the others. He was arrested during a robbery and charged with robbery, use of a weapon, and kidnapping. The kidnapping charge occurred because he had detained the clerk during the robbery. He received five years to life for the kidnapping and another seven to sixteen years concurrently for the robbery. He also received seven to sixteen years for weapons enhancement, and that was not concurrent, meaning he has to serve this second sentence after he is paroled from the first. He has served fifteen years so far in the first sentence and still has not been able to get a parole hearing for the kidnapping. He only has state representation, so there doesn't seem to be any hurry to get a hearing for him.

His mother gave him up to social services for placement in a group home when he was twelve, because she could not control him. He got his GED in juvenile lockup and was there from age thirteen to seventeen. He entered an adult prison at eighteen and served seven years. When he finally got out at age twenty-five, he caught his current case a year later.

He has only spent two years at home since he was twelve years old. He is like a stranger to his sisters, who have very little to do with him. He says they know more about their friends than they do about him, and they only share biology. They have their own lives, children, jobs, and husbands.

Does he have regrets? Sure, he does. He regrets most of his life and the fact that he was not mature enough to realize it the few times when things were good. He does think part of his problems stem from his mother taking him away from his father when he was young, and then putting him in a group home. He says that not only did the group home introduce him to crime, drugs, and violence, but that it also happened when he was feeling abandoned, alone, and scared. His feelings turned to hate, and he hardened. It wasn't until recently that he could even admit how hurt he was. Eventually he realized that although his mother may have made mistakes, she had four kids to take care of, and he was a little jerk and a terror. She may not have known that once she signed custody over, it would be almost impossible to get him back. He does write to her and now they communicate some, but he thinks he reminds her of the mistakes she made, and she seems to feel guilty.

Drugs and alcohol also played a part in it all, although he was not an addict. However, he was either drunk or high each time the police arrested him. All these factors have led to his almost lifelong incarceration. He no longer is a member of a prison gang and seems to have come to terms with what happened, but he has years to go. What hope has he for the future? This is a person who barely had a chance and never learned from any of his incarcerations. He may spend most of the next twenty years in prison; if so, he will be near sixty when he gets out. What in the world can a person who has spent almost his entire life incarcerated do when he is released? I'm not sure there is an answer. I can only hope there will be someone there for him.

Life-course persistent antisocial behavior is thought to begin at an early age and to be a function of brain development.[7] Maybe this partially explains how a person who begins having trouble at an early age persists in their behaviors through adulthood. There are many behaviors and disorders which have been associated with antisocial and criminal behavior, including alcohol abuse, drug abuse, and ADHD. You could also include fetal alcohol syndrome during pregnancy, poor academic ability, low socioeconomic status, poor parenting, and criminality in family members, peers, or parents as contributing factors. At this point there is no formal conclusion, except that the combined factors of genetics and environment lend themselves to long-term criminality. Perhaps a hundred years from now, society may find out that criminals, particularly lifelong criminals, have a different neurological brain structure. As genetics are broken down, we find we are all just composed of little bits

---

7 Terrie E. Moffitt, "Adolescence-Limited and Life-Course-Persistent Antisocial Behavior: A Developmental Taxonomy," *Psychological Review* 100, no. 4 (1993): 674–701, http://www.colorado.edu/ibs/jessor/psych7536–805/readings/moffitt-1993_674–701.pdf.

and pieces all thrown together, and for some of us the pieces just did not fall into the right slots. If those bits and pieces were rearranged, would some of us be geniuses? Would we all be beautiful? Could criminality somehow be eliminated with a little tweak of a laser? What a remarkable achievement that would be for the world.

Thinking about all this, I began wondering if I should try to find Michael's birth parents. Maybe if he met them he could diffuse some of his anger, giving him a better chance at life when he gets out.

Although I had not known who she was in the beginning, I had known his biological mother's name for several years now. The lead attorney who handled the adoption had retired and sent me Michael's folder. In it was a letter from one of the attorneys who oversaw the adoption, and he had mistakenly included her name. Although I had offered to help Michael find his mother in the past, he had always refused. I didn't know if it was fear, anger, or just lack of interest. Because he was older now, I wondered if he had changed his mind on the subject.

Thanks to the Internet, I was able to track her down in a couple of hours. The bigger problem was whether I should call her or not. It looked like she had other children and a husband now. What if they didn't know anything about Michael? What if she didn't want them to know? What gave me the right to interfere with her life after forty-two years?

On the other hand, if I did not call her, I might never know if Michael could take a different path than the one he has followed. Not to say that just finding her would make a miracle happen, but I wondered if it might help him to understand himself. If he found out that she also had problems, he might be willing to let go of some of the guilt he felt when some of the things he did were wrong. I thought perhaps that he might be less angry if he heard from her why she chose to let him be adopted. Maybe he could come to terms with some of his demons. Maybe it would even give me some peace and put doubts I had about any mistakes I made to rest.

In the end, I decided not to call her. I picked up the phone and then set it back down, hearing the tone click off. It sounded soft, like a piece of cloth dropping. I had no right to interrupt her life. After all, she could find him if she wanted to. I had sent several letters to the Nevada Adoption Reunion Registry with the form you can fill out that states you want to contact your biological child or parent. Michael had signed the form years ago, but nothing had ever come of it, so he had stopped thinking she would respond.

Maybe it was better this way. I would let Michael direct the course of his own life.

CHAPTER 30

RECIDIVISM AND RELEASE

My heart beats faster when I think about Michael's upcoming release in three or four years. His release from the federal authorities will complete his obligation to them. However, he still has the state case pending, and we hope he will be able to get parole for that. He is in the process of completing his parole package for the State of Nevada that contains all his school certificates and his educational records, as well as a description of where he will live and how he intends to get a job. He also has to petition his counselor for assignment to a rehabilitation facility or halfway house. Sometimes those facilities are full, so he needs to get a reservation for a room well ahead of time. If Nevada doesn't agree to parole, upon his release from federal custody he will be transferred to a state facility for a yet undetermined period of time.

Ernesto Sirolli, the Italian motivational speaker, once said that in order to motivate someone you must "find out what they want and then help them find a way to achieve it."[8]

Does Michael have a desire or passion for anything? I do not know. I have asked him, but he doesn't seem to know either. The one thing he seems to do well is talk. While he was in AA after being let out of High Desert State Prison, he did a lot of speaking to young people about his life and where it had led him. That is the only thing I have ever known him to be really interested in, except construction work. He would get

---

8 Ernesto Sirolli, "Want to Help Someone? Shut Up and Listen!," transcript and video, 17:09, talk presented at TEDxEQchch, Aurora Centre for the Performing Arts, Christchurch, NZ, August 2012, http://www.ted.com/talks/ernesto_sirolli_want_to_help_someone_shut_up_and_listen.

dressed up in his one and only suit and go to the AA meetings for juveniles. He would tell them about his time at High Desert, and how it had affected him and made his life a nightmare. He would tell them how dangerous prison was and how it felt to be locked up in a six by eight cell all day, every day. He showed them his tattoos and told them about being a member of a gang. It was a story that impressed and scared even the most jaded of the teenagers. When he got home from one of his talks, he would be happy, knowing he had done something good. It was probably the best thing he ever did for them and for himself.

Now he is making efforts to get the Aryan Warriors to let him retire and go free, due to his age and the fact he has hepatitis C and may have future health problems. I can only pray they will let him leave. If they don't give him permission, he will have problems with them after he is released. They will want him to continue to support them. I am nervous and fear for his safety unless they do.

If I am this nervous, how can he be feeling? He has been emailing me more frequently than ever:

Mom, I have to be honest, I am scared about getting out. I will not have been on the outside for almost twelve years by the time of my release. I'm afraid I won't know how to act or what to do. I'm not even sure I can talk to a normal person. I don't have a halfway house assigned yet, and no prospect of a job. I am just hoping you will help me. I know you don't want me to live with you, and I don't want that either. We talked about that on your last visit. But I need help or I'm afraid I will be right back here. I never want to be here again...I would rather be dead, and I'm not kidding about that. I would rather kill myself.

I hope that Michael has reached the point where he can let his common sense override his fear, anger, and embarrassment. If he can figure out what he wants to do when he gets out, then maybe he can get his life together after his release. Maybe he won't fall into all the traps that get so many former inmates sent right back in. All I have ever wanted was for him to have a good life and be happy. Is that too much to ask?

Yet I know the facts; data on recidivism from the US Department of Justice shows that at least 30 percent of parolees commit a crime within the first three to six months of release. Out of all prisoners released in thirty states in 2005, 67.8 percent were arrested within three years of release, and 76.6 percent were arrested within five years of release. The rate of recidivism goes down after five years, but almost 70 to 80 percent of ex-felons return to prison eventually.[9] Having a full-time job helps parolees remain out of prison, though it does not guarantee it. However, just getting that first job is very difficult. Many companies say they hire ex-felons, but there is always fine print with exceptions and reasons for not hiring them. You certainly would not want a child molester working in a day care center, but what difference does it make if a former drug user is working laying block or in construction?

Then there is the reality of life on the outside. When an inmate is ready to be released, they think about all the things they will be able to do and how freedom will feel. A few weeks after they get out, they find that freedom is not as easy as it seemed. The initial feeling of euphoria dies.

They have to report to a parole officer, follow a long list of rules, not associate with other known felons, and provide urine or blood samples for drug testing on request. Slowly the reality of prison wears off, and it becomes easier for them to ignore the rules in favor of what feels good to do. I have seen many heart attack patients follow their diet and exercise

---

9 Matthew R. Durose, Alexia D. Cooper, and Howard N. Snyder, *Recidivism of Prisoners Released in 20 States in 2005: Patterns from 2005 to 2010*, special report (Washington, DC: U.S. Department of Justice, Office of Justice Programs, Bureau of Justice Statistics, April 2014), http://www.bjs.gov/content/pub/pdf/rprts05p0510.pdf.

plans for months, watching their weight, walking, exercising, and not smoking. A year or so later, they have gone back to their old ways. They have forgotten how painful the heart attack was, how close to death they came, and how dangerous it would be for them to have another.

For the parolee, the road back to prison is paved with a series of job rejections and a feeling of not belonging to the community. They drift toward the familiarity and comfort of old friends and old ways. They forget how miserable they were when they were locked up. They forget about the body searches, the lack of privacy, the restrictions, the terrible food, and even the inability to be with their loved ones on the outside. They forget about how calming the ocean is, how mountains look against the sky, or how soft the grass feels on bare feet. They get tired of dealing with all the frustrations, and often find themselves hanging out with the wrong crowd again. They may even think drinking will be okay if they just have one. That may lead to doing just one hit of meth or heroin. From there it is only a matter of time before the police catch them committing a crime, and they are sent back to prison. Their old friends and the guards in the facility are waiting for them, because they have seen it a million times.

If they are in long enough, inmates may become so institutionalized that they do not feel comfortable on the outside, and subconsciously do something to get themselves put back in prison. For those of us who have never been there, it is beyond our comprehension how this can happen. But if we were released with the title of ex-felon, with no skills, no job, no money, no transportation, and no trustworthy, genuine friends, what would our chances be? Probably the same.

That is why it does not make sense to spend somewhere between $15,000 to $60,000[10] a year to house someone, and then spend almost nothing after their release. This cost does not take into consideration all

---

10   Christian Henrichson and Ruth Delaney, *The Price of Prisons: What Incarceration Costs Taxpayers* (New York, NY: Vera Institute of Justice, Center for Sentencing and Corrections, January 2012), http://www.vera.org/sites/default/files/resources/downloads/price-of-prisons-updated-version-021914.pdf.

the costs to the family and to the inmate themselves. Taxpayers are not getting a good return for their money.

Medical doctors working for managed care corporations have incentives in the form of bonuses given to them when they keep patients healthy and out of the hospital. They do not order unnecessary tests, refer to specialists, or hospitalize patients unless it is necessary. Of course, that can backfire for the patient, but for the most part it means people are healthier and happier. The money is now distributed to preventive care so that physicians can address problems before they occur, not after. If the federal government and states would adopt this thinking and spend money to keep parolees out of prison, the debt for institutional care might drop the same way the cost of healthcare drops with preventive care.

The government implemented the federal prison system in 1930. At that time, the system had only fourteen facilities and 13,000 inmates. According to the Bureau of Federal Prisons, as of January 2015 there were over 210,000 inmates.[11] That is just the federal system. According to the Bureau of Justice Statistics, in 2013 there were 1,574,700 prisoners under the jurisdiction of state and federal authorities.[12] Those numbers do not take into consideration any county or city facilities and jails. On March 12, 2014, the Prison Policy Initiative, a criminal justice research advocacy group, reported that there are approximately 2.4 million people in prisons and jails of different types in the United States.[13] The United States has an estimated population of approximately 318,857,056, according to the December 2014 Census Bureau.[14] This means that approximately

---

11   Federal Bureau of Prisons, *Statistics* (Washington, DC: Author, January 22, 2015), http://www.bop.gov/about/statistics/population_statistics.jsp.

12   E. Ann Carson, *Prisoners in 2013*, Report NCJ 247282, (Washington, DC: U.S. Department of Justice, Office of Justice Programs, Bureau of Justice Statistics: September 16, 2014), http://www.bjs.gov/index.cfm?ty=pbdetail&iid=5109.

13   Peter Wagner and Leah Sakala, L., *Mass Incarceration: The Whole Pie* (Northampton, MA: Prison Policy Initiative, March 12, 2014), http://www.prisonpolicy.org/reports/pie.html.

14   United States Census Bureau, *American Fact Finder* (Washington, DC: Author, 2014),http://factfinder.census.gov/faces/tableservices/jsf/pages/productview.xhtml?pid=PEP_2014_PEPANNRES&prodType=table

750 people out of every 100,000 are incarcerated currently. Just a few years ago, the New York Times reported that more than one out of every hundred people in the US was incarcerated in some type of facility.[15] Most countries have an incarceration rate of fewer than 200 per 100,000. The United States has one-quarter of the entire world's incarcerated population while it has only one-fifth of the world's population. What does that say for us?

One of the big problems is that the justice system values punishment over prevention, and this means that they don't prioritize rehabilitative programs or checks and balances. This perpetuates the cycle of even more crime and more punishment. We need to change our perspective on criminal justice to not just retributive punishment, but to include preventive and rehabilitative measures.

One way to make improvements is to make sure the private corporations that are running the prisons for the Bureau of Prisons have checks and balances. There should be financial incentives to rehabilitate and educate inmates and make sure they do not return to prison. Prisoners should all have the opportunity to have a job that teaches them a skill. When they get out, they should be enrolled in programs that not only provide avenues for obtaining a job, but also provide for job training. It is not just about one inmate or one family. It's about an entire system we are all responsible for.

The only way to change this outlook is by getting the word out to the public. They should know how much the penal system is costing them, and how it is not giving a good return on their investment and is not facilitating change for inmates. If the penal system is changed, we will all benefit from it. Jobs and programs will help ex-felons and former inmates stay out of prison. Reduction of penal costs will benefit the taxpayers, and eventually it will result in an improved and safer environment for everyone to live in.

---

15   Adam Liptak, "More than 1 in 100 U.S. Adults Are in Prison, *New York Times*, February 29, 2008, http://www.nytimes.com/2008/02/29/world/americas/29iht-29prison.10561202.html?_r=0.

EPILOGUE

What does the future hold for Michael? I wish I knew. I wish I had a crystal ball and could call up the years yet to follow. Even better, I wish I could direct the future and give it a perfect ending. Will Michael ever become a man who can function in society, who can follow the rules enough to get along in life, hold a job, and earn a living? A man who has friends, comes to family holiday gatherings, and takes responsibility for his children? He tells me he is through with prison, drugs, and crime and absolutely is going to do this. I do not know if he can, but as his mother, I will not let go of that one glimmer of hope. I refuse to give up on him. I will do my best not to be an enabler, but will stand fast and continue to give him tough love. That's all I can do, and I know that.

Most ex-felons don't have a prayer of succeeding, so what are my son's chances? Unless something changes in our penal system to foster change for inmates, those being released will continue to face many difficulties upon release. I can only hope that time and age have made Michael realize that his options are narrow, and that he will have to follow a straight path, adhering to all the rules of society, in order to stay out of prison.

In the end, it is impossible for me to know what the future may bring. All I really know for sure is that I will be at the gate when he gets out, and I will be standing by his side on his journey to freedom.

Time Is There None?
Twisting and turning,
churning,
burning,
Sucked into emptiness,
hold on,
I cannot,
it sees through me.
My thoughts,
my wants,
my needs,
the hopes,
the hates,
as quickly it dissipates,
yet the return inevitable as the darkness of the night itself.
Is the cold embrace of a worm I fear,
I do not know,
Running ever does it get closer,
fighting ever does it get near,
faster,
closer,
closer,
it comes still,
only the quicker I run, the more I fight, it only gets nearer!
Is yet there time or is there none?

Inmate Brett McKeehan, 2005

ACKNOWLEDGMENTS

I sincerely thank the people who have contributed to this book with stories about their own loved ones or their own experiences. It may not have been easy and sometimes may have even been painful, but they have provided me with true and honest feelings, and I am thankful for that. These people include Casey Staker, Pamela Orchow Reeder, Brett McKeehan, and my son, without whom this book would not have been written. I would also like to thank my diligent and supportive editor, Christina M. Frey at Page Two Editing, who took my words and wrestled them into a book I can be proud of. My book cover designer, Morpheus Blak for my compelling and professional cover. Lastly, I have to thank my husband, Lennard Grodzinsky, who supported me through late dinners and a lot of anguish.

SUPPORT SYSTEMS

You are not alone; there are blogs, Facebook pages, support groups, and some state agencies that can help you and your loved one who is incarcerated. This is a partial list of organizations that may provide information and support.

Websites

1. Friends and Family of Incarcerated Persons (FFOIP): http://www.ffoip.org
   FFOIP is a volunteer organization whose focus is to foster community support for the families and children of those incarcerated. They can help with questions you may have; they also try to help when your loved one is set for parole, and keep track of legislative decisions. The main chapter serves the DC area, but there are chapters in other states.
2. Prison Talk: www.prisontalk.com; www.facebook.com/PrisonTalk Community (Facebook page)
   An online community, conceived in a prison cell and designed in a halfway house, it provides a forum for those interested in prisoner support. The aim of this community is to help bring people together so they can find support in their time of need and get their issues and concerns addressed. It also hopes to effect change in the penal system.

3. WriteAPrisoner.com: www.writeaprisoner.com
Communication with the outside world is essential for those who are incarcerated. This website is dedicated to promoting correspondence and facilitating positive change for inmates and citizens. It also has a forum where useful information can be found. They have funded a "Books Behind Bars" program and advocate helping inmates reintegrate back into society.

4. Women's Prison Association: www.wpaonline.org
Women's Prison Association is a service and advocacy organization committed to helping women with criminal histories. It promotes alternatives to incarceration and helps women avoid arrest by making positive changes in their lives. The organization offers help for a variety of problems women may be dealing with.

5. Assisting Families of Inmates (AFOI): www.afoi.org
Dedicated to preventing the breakdown of relationships between inmates and their families, AFOI helps provide regular, meaningful visitation and support, referral, and educational services. Some of their services include help with transportation, children's visitation programs, referrals to other agencies, and information on prison rules and visitation.

6. Prison Activist Resource Center (PARC): www.prisonactivist.org
This prison abolitionist group, based in California, is committed to challenging the prison industrial complex. Their goal is to work with prisoners, ex-prisoners, and their family and friends in order to expose and address the neglect of the more than two million incarcerated persons in the US. A portion of the site is dedicated to resources for inmates and families.

7. The National Resource Center on Children and Families of the Incarcerated: http://nrccfi.camden.rutgers.edu/resources/directory/states
This is a directory of programs serving children and families of the incarcerated. It lists hundreds of helpful organizations by state.

8. Jobs for Felons Magazine: http://www.jobsforfelons.net
A magazine for ex-felons looking for employment. This magazine although primarily located in Seattle, WA provides useful information for job hunting and companies who hire felons. Posts include such information as how to manage money and what jobs felons cannot apply for.

9. Exoffenders, Jobs for Felons and felon friendly employment: https://exoffenders.net/employment-jobs-for-felons
The companies listed on this site do not guarantee jobs for felons; however, the list is updated to include companies that are felon friendly. Each link will lead you to the hiring site for the company.

10. Jobs for Felons: http://www.jailtojob.com/from-jail-job.html
An updated list of companies that hire felons and ex-offenders.

11. Ex-Prisoners and Prisoners Organizing for Community Advancement (EPOCA): www.exprisoners.org
This organization advocates for communities to work together to help people who have paid their debt to society.

12. Prison Culture: www.usprisonculture.com
A blog to provide information about the industrial complex that operates prisons.

13. The Prison Abolition Project: www.facebook.com/Prison AbolitionProject
This Facebook page is dedicated to informing people about the injustice of the prison industry and to advocating for the deconstruction of the system.

14. Friends Beyond the Walls: http://www.friendsbeyondthewall.com
A site that provides photos and personal information of inmates looking for pen pals.

15. www.prisonchat.wordpress.com
Website of the author, offering information and support for friends and families of inmates. This blog addresses all aspects of prisons, supports families and friends of inmates, and discusses a variety of related topics.

Books

1. *Locked Down, Locked Out: Why Prison Doesn't Work and How We Can Do Better* (Maya Schenwar)

   While telling her own family's story, Maya Schenwar speaks to the problems of our penal system, and why it does not work. She examines how prisoners are dehumanized and forgotten in our system. A lot of valuable information can be found in her book, along with suggestions on how we could better deal with the people we are now just warehousing.

2. *Beyond Bars: Rejoining Society After Prison* (Jeffrey Ian Ross and Stephen C. Richards)

   A must for anyone coming out of prison to help prepare for successful reentry, this book gives detailed information on what to expect and how to deal with the problems people run into when they reenter the community.

3. From Jail to Job (Eric Mayo)

   This book is a step by step guide for those who have been incarcerated to find a job. It provides information from how to clean up your rap sheet to how to prepare your resume.

Made in the USA
Middletown, DE
16 June 2015